W9-CMZ-909

The Demand Generation

Customer Managed Relationships

FIRST EDITION

PAUL ANDERSON

Doyle Publishing Company, Inc.

Published by
Doyle Publishing Company, Inc.
5206 FM 1960 West, Suite 107
Houston, Texas 77069 USA
1-800-457-6459
www.doylepublishing.com

Publisher's Cataloging in Publication
Anderson, Paul, 1964-
    The demand generation, customer managed relationships / Paul Anderson.
        p. cm.
        ISBN 0-9653359-6-8   .
        1. Call centers -- Computer network resources.   2. Internet (Computer network)   3. World Wide Web (Information retrieval system)   4. Internet telephony.   5. Customer services. I. Title.

    HE 8788.A64 2001   658.8'4

Cover design by Decoz
Printed in the United States of America
First printing: 2001

SIEMENS

January 2001

We are living in a very interesting time where the Internet is playing an important and meaningful role in everyone's lives. It has revolutionized commerce and business in the US. Traditional Brick and Mortar companies that have invested in communication to embrace the Internet have continued to grow. Through embracing this growing media, enterprises have been able to exchange information and conduct transactions with their customers – businesses and consumers – at an enhanced level of understanding of their market demands.

By our definition "electronic Customer Relationship Management" is the sum of E-Business and CRM. eCRM will extend the same high value service and information offered through traditional customer touch points to new emerging communication media such as the Web and wireless.

As consumer knowledge evolves as fast as the Internet, suppliers must balance velocity and convenience with the benefits of maintaining 1-to-1 relationships. To attain this goal, the need for an eCRM business strategy that will meet the expectations of a demanding generation of informed consumers is mandated.

Paul Anderson identifies the challenges facing business in this dynamic market place in "The Demand Generation". His insight helps the reader understand how communications can be used for competitive advantage and build loyalty between enterprises and customers.

Siemens' strategic offerings in the eCRM worldwide market place are uniquely capable of meeting the demands of allowing this new generation of educated consumers access to and information from the enabled enterprise. As a solutions provider with over 150 years of experience, Siemens brings internationally skilled resources to solve business issues.

With our Compliments

George Nolen

George Nolen

President Siemens EN.

Table of Contents

The Demand Generation
Customer Managed Relationships

However, a sweeping perspective of all industrial technologies shows that in each information-based industry there exists a consistent phenomena in health care-- that the pragmatic application of technology isn't nearly as common as the demonstrable use of technology. Patients don't understand why their banks can go online, but their doctors can't. Interactive health care still has many cultural, legal, and technology hurdles to leap before nearing mainstream. Pure e-health internet plays such as drkoop.com are nearing the end of their life spans, suffering from the agony of now realizing that revenue is much more than a distraction. The actual uptake of "e-health" may in fact be a bit slower than the hype. Like many other business sectors today, media hype far exceeds the true pace of change. E-health, the most personal form of CRM is still in its clinical trial stage.

This emerging generation of customer has a whole new set of behaviors that current technologies simply cannot respond to. This is an internet-powered and knowledge-ified demand generation devoid of segmentation by age. This demand generation has not adopted the internet; they have internalized it. Customers demand comprehensive and accurate information, plenty of choices, competitive prices, and no-strings gimmicks. Companies must realize that they are no longer in the business of implementing technology and managing people, they are in the business of implementing change. Prepare for the future of the ever perpetual change because it is no longer about cost justification, it is about change justification. Can we let go of our Erlangs?

There are two meta-trends influencing the future of computer telephony. The first is the evolution of information as a form of currency where information about transactions becomes more valuable than the transactions themselves. The applications and technology of computer telephony will move away from the efficiencies of transactions as measured by Erlangs to the return on relationships currently represented by CRM. CT will evolve from being efficiency-oriented technology and applications to supporting experience-oriented applications. The second trend is the decentralization of customers, companies, and employees. The change of the endpoints is merging in the decline of the PC and the advent of the wireless devices and networks. Large enterprises will become conglomerations of regional branch offices and remote workers. CTI evolves beyond the confines of a station-

Chapter Seven – Forward Thinkings 59

With Advanstar's permission to reprint, this chapter is a compilation of the 'Forward Thinking' column written from January 2000 to December 2000 for Customer Interface Magazine.

Chapter Eight – Globility and Solutioning 81

The meta-vision of globility and solutioning includes converging the front end of CRM and its back end analytical side with the demands of the smarter mobile enabled customer. From observing CRM disciplines, we can identify a natural evolution toward corporate intelligence combining the thought mining of employee opinions and ideas with the data mining of historical customer data. Looking to the peripheral of call centers, where the pragmatic proof points of CRM can be found, we can identify three significant influences from a technology point of view. The first is globility, which is inclusive of the massive emergent market of wireless applications, particularly WAP (Wireless Application Protocol), and includes the enabling of a distributed workforce, tele-working in particular. The second significant influence is multi-channel customer relationship management; the third is application portability.

Chapter Nine – Succession Networks 93

Call centers are a proof point for the pragmatic application of technology. Networking technology is no exception, particularly within the still vast circuits of voice networking. Few vertical technology issues get so little attention, but have as much of the influence, on the evolutionary pace of technology as that of the emerging next generation of networks. These succession networks will not only carry information, but applications will be added to this dumb glass to create intelligence. This intelligence will now be spread throughout the entire customer demand chain tremendously affecting how, where, and when enterprises interact with their customers. Understanding the true nature and underestimated impact of these emerging succession networks inevitably ends up changing conventions on how we think the applications of technology will affect customer service.

Chapter One
Return on Relationship

Abstract

It is the emerging internet-knowledgeified customers that are demanding the greater return on their relationships. A clear demand from this generation of customers is that companies shift their concentration from transaction-based service to relationship-based engagements. The generation of this demand is forcing companies to rethink whole new types of business behaviors.

The supreme market advantage of ROR is that it can be a tipping point in the advancement toward relinquishing the grip of traditional customer satisfaction and its Erlang-related metrics in the CRM game. Ideas such as gaining a return on a relationship are based on the assertion that what used to work— Erlang for example—does not work anymore. Return on relationship—ROR—fundamentally contradicts the transactional efficiencies most enterprises strive to achieve today. You no longer want to work to shorten the engagement with customers; you want to lengthen it.

Transitioning from the industrial Erlang to ROR reflects the obvious larger and more dramatic e-market evolution. Return on relationships is a concept designed to express the evolution from seeking transactional efficiencies to the new opportunities of gaining customer loyalty.

In fact, Customer Relationship Management—CRM—would insult the average customers if they knew about it. CRM is a very nice little acronym that does not really describe accurately what customers truly want. Customers don't want to be managed. Customers manage relationships now. The Demand Generation is about customers demanding control of their relationships with you, not the other way around.

Flying with Peasants

I live in Houston and I fly Continental Airlines almost everywhere I go. Houston is a hub for Continental and I live near a high-speed beltway that is only 28 minutes from garage to gate. Like a few others, I have also flown enough miles this year on Continental Airlines that I made Platinum Elite level in August. When you fly as often as I do, the little advantages of being recognized as a frequent flyer become important.

Upgrading and flying in first class is definitely something frequent flyers have been known to do battle over, because after the first time you have been upgraded and you have flown in first class, you never want to fly with the peasants again.

Several years ago, I only flew 45,000 miles in one year with Continental. This was 5,000 miles short of achieving the Gold Elite status. Among other significant perks, Gold Elite is the status that allows you the opportunity to upgrade to first class two days in advance.

At the same time, I have a friend who owns a first-class moving company. That year he flew less than 20,000 miles on Continental Airlines. Continental also gave him Gold Elite status. This was annoying— why him and not me? Because most every time he flew on Continental, he paid for several of his crewmembers to go with him. Continental didn't give him Gold status because he traveled; they gave him Gold status because he bought plenty of tickets.

Continental Airlines, like many companies, may be missing the boat— rather, the flight—here. Because while Continental may be achieving a high ROI on my moving-company friend, they may be missing out on a very high return on a relationship with me.

Somewhere in a cubicle near Continental Airlines' headquarters is an MBA person with a calculator who has calculated the likely value of my business over my lifetime, my lifetime customer value.

Continental Airlines has the opportunity to recognize, through constant dialog, that while I am not a high-dollar value customer measured in miles flown, I am certainly a high-influence customer, a luminary customer. The difference between a return on an investment (ROI) and a return on a relationship (ROR) is that while your MBA has done a good job of monetizing my value as a customer, he may have completely missed my value as an influencer.

My lifetime value, according to Lexus, is around $600,000. It turns out that Lexus, when considering my lifetime value, knows that there is no way my wife would ever let me buy $600,000 worth of luxury automobiles over any amount of lifetime. $600,000 is an awful lot of cars and service for a single customer.

But what Lexus is also considering in their relationship value equation is the influence, or the loss of influence, by loyal customer segments. It is not just the buying power of any individual that adds up to $600,000, it is the buying power of the many other individuals that one may influence that creates the $600,000 value.

How do you identify my value as a customer with influence?

Just ask me.

Information is the currency of the digital age. As technology evolves, every company will keep track of each and every dialogue it has with its customers. In every transaction and interaction there is a great deal of information customers reveal about themselves and their buying habits, volunteering information within their individual comfort levels. It will be the information gleaned from those conversations and engagements that will truly drive the building of loyal, long-term returns and profitable relationships. The more knowledge you have about your customers, the more wealth your company will have.

Today, your company theoretically has the ability to identify each population of customers that have a disproportionate influence unrelated to their fiscal value. This is called the Pareto Customer, after Alfredo Pareto, an Italian that came up with the core of the 80/20 rule. The Pareto customer is the one whom we are after—more specifically, the Pareto complainer. Frequent flier and frequent car renter programs are a modern manifestation of the Pareto Principle.

Then there is the more tangible phenomena in which the increase in customer retention accounts for x% increase in revenues and profits. I think it is the first time that we had heard a customer articulate influence as a key part of their relationship strategy. Taking into account the value of the luminary customer, there is recognition of the value of a customer being so much more than the calculation of the dollars they spend.

It is ironic that the most loyal customers are the ones that are the most unsatisfied. If you don't get involved and listen to what they have to say, and instead focus on measuring how long those conversations last, you are missing the opportunity to capture information as valuable as any currency. We used to create products and services for customers; now they are telling us exactly what they want us to do. But we are not listening to them because we are more interested in getting customers off of the phone than we are in finding out what they want. We are better at picking their pockets than picking their brains.

There are thousands of companies with millions of customers like you and me all over the world now.

In the industrial age, customer satisfaction was measured as a return on transaction, or ROI—Return on Investment. Like most every other business figure, ROI was measured in the industrial economy through a rear view mirror. Things such as satisfaction were measured by what had already happened between the customer and the company. They were old news. In the industrial economy we are in, all projects are based on Return on Investment

Today, no one questions the business objective of being able to attract, retain, and grow customers through any means; the customers want to do business seamlessly. This includes engagements handled over the phone, over the web, in person, via snail mail, eventually video, or through a call center.

In the future, if you could have this greater network out there, that is really now enabling the extended enterprise. What is at the heart of this? It is the need to know what is happening with your customers and what is happening within the business with your relationships. How do you hold your partners accountable? What if you must depend on partners to actually deliver service capabilities that achieve customer loyalty and metrics as well? All of this information becomes more and more important in transactions that become more and more faceless.

The efficiencies we are squeezing out of service and measuring with things such as customer satisfaction may be costing us more than we think.

It is the emerging internet-knowledgeified customers that are demanding the greater return on their relationships. A clear demand from this generation of customers is that companies shift their concentration from transaction-based service to relationship-based engagements. The generation of this demand is forcing companies to rethink a whole new type of business behaviors. New engagement behaviors such as ROR are not about looking beyond the transaction or set of transactions, but the profoundness of the influence factor as well. When a company looks ahead at its customers' needs, preferences and demands, then customers begin to feel vested in that company and the company gains a whole new brand of loyal customer. Fulfilling customer demands makes for loyal customers who are profitable customers.

To protect their investment in customers as they evolve over time—even over generations—savvy companies will concentrate on exploiting the value of their customers over longer and longer periods of time.

21st century companies will build relationships, engagement by engagement, as customers shift in age, interests, spending patterns and every other

4

demographic possibility.

The speed of business today demands that companies recognize and capitalize on unique shifts in their customers' demographics—life style changes that would influence the value of those relationships. Getting a return on customer relationships is about developing a strategy that understands how customer needs and preferences evolve over time, not in the context of a single transaction.

With mass media as worthy accomplices, surprisingly many companies today still throw out big nets like television and radio commercials to gain as many customers as they can with little or no thought to the idea of just keeping the customers they already have and charging them more. I will pay more for companies that love me.

Many companies are still operating under the industrial age thinking embodied in notions of average speed of answer, abandonments, Erlangs, and customer satisfaction levels. All of which, as goals we strive to accomplish in customer relationships, are dead. Today, customer satisfaction is at the bottom of the list as a bare minimum requisite just to remain in business. Customer satisfaction is just the price of entry into the customer charged economy; it alone cannot provide the profits that a return on relationships can.

In the industrial model, there are fulfillment, value, convenience, trust, then customer satisfaction. In the new world model, customer satisfaction is at the bottom, then you have to bond with your customer, then you have to personalize it—personalization—then you have empowerment, in which the relationship is two-way; the customers are empowered to tell you what they want or they empower you act on their behalf. Finally, there is customer loyalty at the top.

The 175-Year Grip of Erlang

There is a good chance that we may look back at some point and identify that the idea of a return on customer relationships was the market tipping-point in the relinquishing of the grip of traditional measures of customer satisfaction and transactional efficiencies.

Unless customers request, want, or even demand shorter phone calls and transaction times, metrics and algorithms that measure efficiency, such as Erlang, will increasingly no longer work. Ideas such as gaining a return on a relationship are based on the assertion that what used to work—Erlang for example—does not work anymore. Erlang is a traditional inward measure and future measures of success less and less include the influence of an Erlang.

The Erlang algorithm itself is a derivative of a formula used during the

Napoleonic Wars to calculate how many cannon and cannon ball were needed to efficiently kill as many of the enemy as possible. From there, we went to calculating how many phone lines a village would need to connect to the next larger town. Now call centers depend on Erlang to calculate how few agents can answer how many customers that will stay on hold for as tortuously long as possible.

It is no coincidence that call centers today are heavily skewed toward measuring efficiencies when we discover that most call centers are found in the CFO's line of command and control. Once an enterprise recognizes that a fundamental challenge in traditional customer service functions, measuring things such as customer satisfaction, is a poor way to measure success, then a broader and more unifying concept of a return on relationship can come into play.

Unlike even CRM, return on relationships is more inclusive than realizing supra-efficiencies—ROIs—in call centers. In fact, return on relationship—ROR—fundamentally contradicts the transactional efficiencies most enterprises strive to achieve today. You no longer want to work to shorten the engagement with customers; you want to lengthen it.

Transitioning from the industrial Erlang to ROR reflects the obvious larger and more dramatic e-market evolution. Return on relationships is a concept designed to express the evolution from seeking transactional efficiencies to the new opportunities of gaining customer loyalty. Call centers, being so heavily dependant on Erlang, will see the most dramatic impact as they prepare to talk longer to customers who are demanding more than ever.

Technology Enables Discrimination

One of the most profound impacts of the internet today is the knowledgeification of customers. Customers often now know more about your company's products and services than the very people within your company to whom they talk. Technology, as a consequence, enables discriminating customers. Customers are more demanding because they know more about you and tell more people today than they ever have been able to before. Customer relationships are dynamic. They are two-way; the internet guarantees that.

The discrimination exercised by customers as to with whom and when they will do business isn't a simplistic one based on price alone. There is a set of values and things that are important to the customer such as flexibility, live person availability, convenience, etc.—things that I, as a customer, am willing to pay a little more for.

In today's e-market place, where everything in the world can be distilled down to a web page, the only differentiation that a company has is price and this is not a sustainable interest to people. At some point, people are going to know that they don't want to be a part of this narrow minded pricing market relationship. In this space, the only way to position yourself is to lower your price.

The drive of technology, from a solutions perspective, is that customers can now pick companies based on their needs, not just simply on criteria such as cost or price. Price will no longer be the most important consideration to the customer.

In fact, Customer Relationship Management—CRM—would insult the average customers if they knew about it. CRM is a very nice little vendor acronym that does not really describe accurately what customers truly want. Customers don't want to be managed. Customers manage relationships now. The Demand Generation is about customers demanding control of their relationships with you, not the other way around.

For example, customers increasingly look at the "social consciousness" of the companies they do business with. Many companies know that there are potential opportunities to do business with populations of customers that make decisions based on mutual objectives and values. How do you find those customers that will make more of their loyalty decisions based on these types of criteria? When companies start asking what things are important to their customers, not just their age, sex and color preferences, they begin to gain value in the form of information. Then questions about personalization emerge, which brings into this equation questions such as what are the things the customer values— what is really important to the customer? What kinds of decisions and desires do I want to do business with?

It's a bit simplistic, but when the company begins to brand for relationships and not for price, you gain those loyal customers who are willing to pay more. Likewise, when you move from just satisfaction toward long-term loyalty, you find customers will also pay more. Loyal customers are more profitable over time and are more likely to refer new customers—a key factor in lowering the cost of acquiring new customers.

Loyal customers are also more likely to follow your company through product discontinuities and into new product lines and services. Companies that foster customer loyalty and constantly evolve to meet new customer needs are the ones that never obsolete themselves.

Loyalty is a function of a high return on relationships. A better ROR leads to a better ROI, not the other way around. In a hierarchy driven by a return on relationships, customer satisfaction is subordinated to customer loyalty. Loyalty is the pinnacle of the new world ROR pyramid. A high ROR has a correlation with high customer loyalty. A higher ROR equates to a higher customer loyalty.

In the future, customers will identify for you exactly what they need and then they will expect companies to figure out how best to deliver it to them and meet their needs. The emergence of the internet has insured that the most powerful form of advertising today is not just word of mouth, but word of web. When customers begin to brag about their loyalty, not just their satisfaction, these are the customers you want.

This whole idea of gaining customer loyalty in the age of the discriminating customer leads to questions about how best to implement customer loyalty strategies at a less expensive rate. While the internet customers tend to be more discriminating than ever before, technology has enabled companies to be discriminating as well.

Discriminating Companies

Companies want to do this, but they don't want to verbalize that there are some customers they want to fire—wishing the competition would get them. This is the conflict between old world marketing and new world marketing. We are used to throwing big nets and getting as many customers as we can and sorting them out later, now we can target and get the right fish, not all fish.

And the internet also enables discriminating companies. Because, now that we have the technology to keep track of these things, customers can always be defined as being a segment of a demographic group as small as one. When you brand customers on a basis of one, you can ultimately move to pricing discrimination that is based on personality characteristics. For example, obnoxious whiners should be charged more than passively loyal customers. Demanding customers cost more.

When we think about segmenting customers we know that not all customers are created equal. Today, companies create offerings and we do marketing campaigns around these offerings. Tomorrow, the offerings will be tailored on the fly, dynamically. Instead of taking months and years of people time, not lapsed time, to set up customer relationships, they will be spontaneously formed, and broken, in days and hours.

Technology does give control and the power to discriminate to the enterprise as well. Flexibility is the ability to identify and respond to a whole set of customer needs that have come up that are not necessarily ongoing but are relevant at the time because it makes good business sense. An enterprise may want to strike up a partnership around a particular customer segment that it normally wouldn't do business with depending on inventory levels, as an example. Then we can identify when a particular customer or segment happens to be using the highest resources.

If the caller that you are sending to automation happens to be the wife of the president of the company (a stakeholder), you might want to schmooze a little because she would have an identifiable influence. Why don't companies recognize their shareholders? If I own stock in Continental Airlines, shouldn't I get preferential treatment as often as a once a year accidental traveler?

Airlines need not only to be able to identify their Gold and Platinum customers, but what about upgrading other worthy stakeholders such as shareholders, or perhaps other Elite class members from competitors?

What is ROR? ROR is an Algorithm

Return on relationship began as a technology application philosophy, a modus operandi. If you buy into the idea that customer loyalty with the right customers leads to a better bottom line and higher profits, then moving forward you need to consider the influence of obtaining a return on customer relationships to justify your customer strategy.

ROR is a philosophy that forces the question, is it customer satisfaction you are looking for or is it customer loyalty you are striving for? ROR is not, as a philosophical tenet, easy to discuss with simplistic acronyms such as CRM, ERP, CTI and XYZ.

What is unique about the idea of ROR is that it is a philosophy that has metrics and tools behind it, whereas most other philosophies don't or are likely just metrics and tools themselves.

ROR is basically an algorithm and methodology based on a set of variables with weights assigned to those variables. Each company discriminates by defining a particular set of variables and assigning a weight for each variable. The weights are subjective at their core and ultimately this scoring depends on whoever is responsible for running the system. The weighting by company or by segment can be, and will be, different. There ends up being an index. The index calculates the sum of the variables times the weight.

For example, suppose a list of ROR variables included the following: revenue from sales, revenue influenced, margin from sales over the total interaction expenses, and the number of high margin expenses. Also included can be variables for call center talk time, the cost of talk time, internet purchases, and face-to-face—all of the different types of touch points. An increasingly important but complex variable is the ratio of problems solved by self-help services versus the use of call center representatives. The concept of return on relationships is designed around the idea of weighting those variables based on any particular target segment of customer. The variable list can theoretically get quite large.

Marketing analytics is the emerging discipline that defines and weights business variables and customer interaction results. Now a series of reports, both real time and historical, can be generated and, for example, a call center manager can identify where they are with customer segmentation and how they are doing on their quest for customer loyalty.

The Pace of the Race

People slow down on freeways because they can't see what's next and they are depending on their partners, the other freeway drivers, to de-futurize for them. No one should expect their partners to be right about something that far ahead in the future, but they can expect them to be confident.

There is a tremendous difference between knowing what is next and knowing how fast what's next gets here. It is the pace of the race that we must understand in order to time success. The pace of web years demands that we have to look at the world, at least as it relates to the software and technology business, in one year to 18 month intervals. When you look back 18 months and imagine the snapshot of the world then and now look at how much the world has changed since, you see the point.

However, progress does not happen fast everywhere at once. For example, in call centers today, the fact is that less than 30 percent of companies have yet to put in CTI applications more complicated than screen pop. The idea that people are actually buying CRM, much less CTI or SFA—whatever they are—is driven by the notion that when an industry reaches between 15 and 20 percent of penetration, we stop doing tradeshows and producing magazines about it. That the idea of CRM is still of any interest to anybody means that there is a very slim percentage of the population actually doing it.

If you believe the full-page Wall Street Journal ads, you are lead to believe that half of the world, in terms of the Fortune 5000, has implemented the sophistications of CRM, SFA, ERP and CTI, and even more likely, are actually realizing any benefits.

Not only does the hype far exceed the true rate of change, but the hype is more along the lines of what needs to be done, meaning that what we are seeing and hearing today is just a road map, subject to change, for 18 months or so from now. Convergence has not really happened. We are at the very beginnings. If you were to draw the life cycle of the generation and communication of this value proposition, we are most definitely still in the infancy stage.

The pervasive customer relationship happens when we all talk about managing every customer touch point, every engagement and every interaction and personalized selling and service transparency for the customer via the phone or the web. These are all technologies that are available today, but companies embracing this stuff are actually back on square one themselves.

The customer relationship technology market is no different than many other economy sectors. CTI, CRM, SFA and ERP are proof points that vendors are overwhelming the market place with more features, like Microsoft has done with *Word* or *Excel*.

It is a very underestimated observation, but the most significant thing that Microsoft ever did with *Word* wasn't in creating helpful paperclips, it was to connect *Word* to *Excel, PowerPoint, Outlook* and other applications. Microsoft's greatest accomplishment was not in creating thousands of features for their products, but in the integration of the products all working together—the "suite" phenomena.

The challenge today is that all of the technologies and applications and processes that we have in our enterprises don't work together. The CTI, CRM, IVR, ERP and SFA are full of features, but don't function together at all. The challenge to companies that want to practice customer discriminating today is that all of the applications, interfaces, devices, and technologies that are supposed to connect your company to customers, don't.

When we talk about the technologies facing customers and employees alike, two or three years from now, this CRM thing has got to be as pervasive as everybody logging into Office or Windows or MyYahoo to get their stock quotes every day. Well traveled functions only need to work usably, very much in a connected fashion, in a user friendly form factor and make these things high performance, secure and reliable.

Otherwise we will end up with an organization called the e-business organization that continues to be the sole center of the universe when it comes to articulating and delivering this message—and this won't scale. Pervasive is when the market has found a way to get this to the masses.

Most importantly, a return on relationships is realized when every employee can log into the state of the customer. Return on relationships drives the development of having Windows or Office on your desktop. It becomes pervasive.

Then you introduce the kinds of connectivity of wireless telephony and voice and you introduce the fact that business professionals will no longer be lugging around ten pound laptops a year from now, that they will be using a WAP device or PDA that is connected all of the time. When you consider voice and speech recognition and synthesis technology, we can all see the potential for huge breakthroughs.

ROR - the Future

It is much too early to tell if the concept of a return on relationships will have sticking power in the market. There are an awful lot of vernacular, acronyms, buzzwords and slogans masquerading as strategy in the market today. Although the concept of gaining a return on relationships is profound, it must still have the stamina to rise above market noise. People in general do not change their interfaces, devices, and acronyms quite as quickly as the media would have us believe.

Further, not only must the idea of a return on relationships rise above market noise, it must also beat back the entrenched and reflexive behaviors developed around obtaining efficiencies and customer satisfaction.

If the battle is to be won, a philosophy of return on relationships must be elevated and that Erlangs fundamentally contradicts what return on relationships is all about must be recognized. As a vestige of the Napoleonic era, Erlang is a traditional inward measure and future measures of success do not include Erlang. Gaining a return on a relationship is based on the idea that what used to work—Erlang for example—does not work anymore.

The supreme market advantage of ROR is that it is likely to be a tipping point in the advancement toward relinquishing the grip of traditional customer satisfaction and its Erlang-related metrics. In today's world, most customer service measurements are a derivative of some form of return on investment. In the new customer charged economy, customer satisfaction becomes the measure at the bottom of the customer food chain.

Customer satisfaction is not the only game we are playing here. Just satisfying customers is easy; it is blowing customers away that creates loyalty. If companies are not providing high levels of customer satisfaction moving forward, they are not going to be in the game. Customer satisfaction becomes the ante required just to play in the game. Customer loyalty is the ultimate goal.

Tomorrow, customer relationships will be dynamically formed. These customer/company relationships will be dynamically formed and created depending on different factors. The difference is that the customer, not the company, will determine loyalty.

At its core, return on relationships—ROR—is more about the seamless customer experience than we have ever considered before. ROR is a very dynamic, ever-changing concept that will change with the future.

One of the most promising facets of ROR is that not only is it philosophically sound, but it also provides an entire new set of analytic tools and metrics that can indicate whether or not you are achieving the quest for customer loyalty, not just merely satisfaction.

Inertia is a powerful force. Technology today enables the knowledgeifi-cation of customers and the ability for companies to discriminate customers based on their value at that moment. This is quite different than being efficient at managing the technology that they use to access your company. Part of the vision must include the pragmatic realization that customers are picking companies as much as companies think that they are picking customers.

The return on relationships vision thing, as it relates to discriminating, knowledgeified, and demanding customers today, clearly unifies many of the service demands customers will increasingly have as we move into the information age.

Chapter Two
The Demand Generation Imperative

The industrial age was spent increasing and maximizing the efficiencies of business, enterprise, commerce, and supply chains. Today, after 250 years or so, an immense and fundamental shift is happening as companies move from being excellent at supply chain management to being excellent at the demand side of the equation.

The emerging information age is about companies focusing on the demand side of the enterprise formula—the customers—not only who they are but also what they want and how they want to interact with the companies they want to do business with.

A recent survey done by The Aberdeen Group revealed that 93 percent of all CEOs ranked satisfying and retaining customers as one of the most critical factors to the success and competitiveness of their companies. For several years now, the market has known that it costs five to ten times more to acquire a new customer than it costs to retain an existing customer. Bain & Co. reaffirms that a mere five percent improvement in customer retention can increase profitability by 25 to 100 percent. The consequences of these three accelerating factors drives market leaders to a realization that future profits are to be found in the retention of profitable customers.

For several generations, companies have been successful at managing the customer experience through a handful of one-way channels such as the telephone, television and newspapers. Concentrated and intense focus on the customer experience and customer satisfaction is a latent development in the change of strategic level business philosophies over the past several generations.

Now the internet has changed this dynamically and along several new dimensions. In fact, the internet has proven to be the tipping point for many emergent technology application sectors, including managing the channels of customer demand.

In the past, superior customer service was often a consequence of implementing technology to create efficiencies. Superior customer service was marketed as an afterthought and technology was used to gain often extraordinary efficiencies out of transactions—quite the opposite of today.

The internet is one of the most dramatic drivers of change society has ever seen. Its impact rivals that of the book, the television, and the telephone as a medium. Its two most profound impacts are that not only does it create more knowledgeable customers, it enables them to interact in dramatic—and often unexpected—new ways.

The internet empowers people with an availability of information such as the world has never seen before. As a consequence, customers often know more about a company's products and services than the very people at the company with whom they talk. Customers certainly often know more about competitive offerings, discounts, and promotional offerings than the customer service agents themselves, in most companies.

The traditional boundaries between the buyers and the sellers are breaking down more quickly than anyone could have ever imagined. The internet in particular is forcing businesses to streamline their processes, open new markets and create agile and flexible information-driven environments that adapt quickly to customer demands.

An unmistakably critical component of this demand generation is technology. However, technology and its applications do not, in and of themselves, create demand—they vary it. The internet is forcing enterprises to become adept at managing the diverse interactions of customer demand.

Customer demand for more channels is a demand for more choices. A single, or even a handful of channels, simply can no longer serve customers effectively. Customers are determining the method of communication. For example, a business not having the ability to chat with customers while they are on the company web page has proven to be costly.

Enterprises today, regardless of industry, must meet or exceed their customer demands for choices in how they purchase products, request and receive service, and access information by providing them with the required support whenever and however they choose it. Every enterprise today is similarly struggling with an emerging conflict between the channels that customers want to use and the channels the company has available.

The internet has enabled a demand generation that wants rich, contextual information that is easy to search and navigate, even if this means making a human being available to help. Expectations of customer experiences by customers are set from places companies could never have imagined just several years ago. It is often from leading companies entirely outside an industry that competitive pressure comes from. Customers expect 24 hours, seven days a week instant availability to information and resources because everybody else seems to try to provide it.

Companies that see and act on the inevitability of multi-channel customer interaction management including, phone, voice mail, email, instant messaging and chat, voice over IP, web call back, and other customer optimization applications will realize greater profits and sustainable competitive futures. Particularly astute companies are adopting a blended business model in which the internet reinforces already existing and developed channels such as direct sales and contact centers.

A new, comprehensive meta-level description is emerging for the meaningful way technology is applied to empower consistent customer experiences.

This chapter discusses the challenges and benefits of managing the interactions of customer demand. Not only is managing the generation of these demands difficult, the generation of customer that is creating these demands is also becoming more diverse and complex. Customer service was already supported by complex fragile environments with high initial capital and operating costs. Unfortunately, today this is even more so.

Managing the Interactions of Customer Demand

Competition, especially among internet-based commerce enterprises, has resulted in razor thin margins and fierce competition for existing environments. Any hope for profitability in the e-commerce endeavor can only come from the realization that not only do companies need to capture the mind share and loyalties of their customers, but that they have to retain them as well. Getting a grip on this customer is about as easy as getting a grip on a slippery fish and it is not getting any easier because the fish is getting slipperier.

Technology, in and of itself, does not change or improve the customer experience. It is the business strategy behind the technology that enables the consistently satisfying customer experience. Customer interactions and engagements should occur seamlessly. When they don't, the customer notices and the enterprise often does not know about it. A consistent customer experience happens when a company's www.com address has the same expectations as the company's 800 number does.

As a consequence, the internet has forced companies to focus more on customer interactions. In competitive price environments, the only distinguishing characteristic customers can identify and recognize about companies today is superior customer experience. Unfortunately for business, customer expectations about experiences change. This makes the ability to deliver consistent customer experiences a competitive advantage. In the future, the greater competitive value will be found in delivering to customers not only consistent, but continuously improving customer experiences.

Extraordinarily high customer satisfaction with a fax-back application may be masking the fact that relatively more valuable customers are trying to reach the customer interaction center by cellular phone and likely do not have the time to wait in a queue for twenty minutes.

There are two known components to successful customer interaction management. The first is a consistent interaction across all media. The second component is the companies that provide the specific knowledge as it applies to specific customers.

Optimizing for Pareto

Strategically thinking enterprises are devoting much more time and resources to thinking deeply about how to identify, discriminate, and retain the most profitable customers.

The 18th century economist Vilfredo Alfredo Pareto introduced the idea of the 80/20 principle. The Pareto Principle suggests that twenty percent of every enterprise's customers will account for eighty percent of the revenue. The Pareto Principle is the basis for frequent flyer and frequent member programs. Identifying and managing this high lifetime value customer is the basis on which the entire one-to-one and lifetime value marketing depends.

The one-to-one influence has been appreciable. By a ratio exceeding three-to-one, enterprises rate customer retention and expansion of their business with existing customers as more important than expanding market share by acquiring new customers. The ideal end is that the company optimizes every engagement based on the Pareto value of the customer.

Optimizing customers requires not only the analytical ability to back-sight customer relationships, but maybe more importantly the ability to project—forecast into the future—anticipated behaviors, needs and preferences of customers.

Ongoing dialogues are the only way to understand how customer needs, desires and preferences are evolving over time. Customer intelligence comes from the customer information the company has an opportunity to gather with every engagement. A form of loyalty based on operational entanglement occurs when companies track customer preferences from transactions over time. With each engagement, theoretically, the relationship between a customer and the enterprise should become deeper.

Every customer engagement can be optimized for that unique customer's demand. Customer optimization is in the segregating of customer and stakeholder segments with complete discrimination based on their value, profitability, and resource demands. Today, the market of solutions for optimizing customer demand can be generally defined around CRM, although an inspection of the CRM market clearly leaves out the vital customer interaction management piece. Practical applications of personalization—or optimization—include customizing personal content, advertising, and even website layout.

Optimizing customers is found in the best companies who concentrate more of their resources on their Pareto customers and create more cost-efficient offerings for less valuable customers. When the company has a clear understanding of the value of customer resources they can accurately and efficiently allocate those resources to provide premium service to those specific customer segments.

Customer demand and interaction management are not only the uses of technology to identify the customer, but also to be aware of the customer's entire history with the enterprise in order to preferentially treat that customer according to rules residing in a corporate knowledge database. This means it is important to understand the challenge of providing a consistent customer experience—a company does not make the mistake of treating a $100,000 customer perfectly when they call on the telephone and then treat them like a $2 customer over the internet.

This represents a broad, sweeping and difficult corporate-wide objective. Proof of the importance of the demand generation imperative is a new corporate executive officer position titled Chief Customer Officer. Meta Group anticipates that 25 percent of multinational companies will have and will fill this Chief Customer Officer position by 2003.

It is a fundamental element of human nature to want to do business with companies that know and want to understand how their customers' needs, preferences and desires are changing over time. People will do business with companies that want to do business with them. Some companies have even successfully met the needs, desires and preferences of customers for multiple generations. This is the type of loyalty that providing enriched customer experiences will generate. The Pareto customer is loyal, stays longer, and spends more money in the long run.

Without question, customer satisfaction and loyalty are the most critical elements of a successful and enduring corporate strategy. In markets today, cost is no longer a mitigating factor. Companies will be competitive in their markets by being the most effective with the interactions of customer relationships.

Technology's Challenges

The challenge of deploying and implementing customer-facing technology today is that there is just so much of it and it is changing so quickly. In the onrush of the information age, many enterprises have entrenched defensively. It is not uncommon to find that enterprises have spent tens of thousands—often millions of dollars—integrating multiple systems and multiple complex custom databases, only to later realize that the idea of managing customer relationships is much more profound than the solutions offered in CRM suites available today.

To date, most investments in customer relationship technology have been in the pursuit of efficiency in transactions. Even state-of-the-art contact centers, sophisticated sales force tools, and complex marketing analytics can, and often do, create extraordinary efficiencies, but these technology applications in total may not be that effective.

Technology disparity can be found where huge investments in accounting and ERP systems, business reprocess engineering, just-in-time manufacturing and logistics have been made. Noticeably common today is that the sophisticated ERP/CRM applications and capabilities many of the companies have adopted are often deployed in such disparate configurations that integrations are rarely effective. In fact, the market is growing leery of the CRM unfulfillments.

There are many examples of application disparity disruptions. Reporting in typical customer contact center environment is one. The disparate technology issue is a standard problem in most every customer interaction center today. In the traditional customer contact center environments, enterprises have multiple reporting, recording, monitoring, and administration points. This creates systemic challenges with not only accuracy, but efficiency as well.

In terms of system accuracy, the typical customer contact center creates reports at the end of every business day, if not more often. For example, a typical report will detail the number of hours worked by a customer service agent who is involved in both an inbound and an outbound campaign. It may suggest that the customer service agent worked for five hours taking customer telephone calls and a separate report will detail that the very same agent then spent four hours making outbound telephone calls. It appears as though he has been working for nine hours engaging customers. When training, breaks, and meetings with supervisors are factored in, intuitively the report metrics do not add up coherently.

In these environments, an enterprise must pool reports on employee productivity and customer interaction process efficiencies. Email, outbound dialers and IVR all typically have different report formats, vernacular and nomenclatures. This is often cumbersome and difficult to manage.

Supervisors and managers of contact centers depend significantly on reporting and metric structures. The advantage of enabling a multitude of enterprise wide views of activity can best be gained when the access and availability of reports is found on a single engine.

A company cannot take strategic systems and put them on top of disparate system architectures found in nearly every company today and implement business rules. Customer experiences cannot be dynamically delivered in these environments. Systemic of application disparity creates lost value from never fully integrating the silos and stacks of enterprise knowledge and information. Enterprises that understand the competitive advantage of leveraging customer information across the entire customer demand and retention process will profit.

Today's customer interaction environment demands some form of blended function—universal agents. The internet today is only creating more complexity. This complexity significantly impacts enterprise productivity if not managed correctly.

Today's technologies of customer interactions, such as intelligent network routing, speech recognition, web IVR, predictive dialing and complex peripherals, all add an additional layer and requires a "glue," which is typically a computer telephony (CTI) layer, to try to blend multiple different systems. The fact is that the fragility of the entire system has increased.

Unfortunately, when it comes to consistent customer relationships, the greater the system disparities, the greater the degradation of the customer experience. The channels that the internet alone has enabled, such as email, have created significant reordering of customer expectations about the fulfillment of consistent service-using technology. Consistent customer experiences begin with consistent technology. There are many reference points in the enterprise where disparate systems create disruptions.

The Role of the Traditional Customer Interaction Center

Traditional semi-asynchronous customer engagement channels included the telephone, fax, mail and IVR. Today the internet has enabled a whole new set of media, including email, web callback, instant messaging, voice over IP and shared browsing. Bandwidth that ultimately enables television quality video engagements is not so far in the distant future.

The customer interaction center—call center—is a very complex and fragile environment. What used to be a fairly typical "call center" operation, primarily juggling agent resources, is now faced with the challenge of adding email servers, web collaboration servers, voice over IP gateways, and complex IP applications.

A significant influence on the uptake and adoption of customer related technology is the increasing need for retaining better-trained customer service agents. Along with significant upgrades in technology must come a reciprocal upgrade in skill sets. Sophisticated technology demands better trained agents, an expensive resource for more enabled customers.

While voice is, and will remain for some time, the preferred, and thus primary, channel of customer communication, email is quickly gaining in popularity with a broad range of companies and consumer segments. Email management is a critical piece of any company's strategic customer related initiatives. Web callback and instant messaging are steadily gaining in market preference and are already an important part of any customer related technology growth. The point here, and one that will discussed several times in this book, is that the traditional function of a call center does not go away.

A proof point of the efficacy of the voice channels is revealed with a closer examination of e-commerce companies such as Amazon.com, webvan, priceline.com, Dell, and Gateway. While their internet operations are getting all of the attention, it is their call centers that are doing all of the work.

According to a study by the GartnerGroup titled, "Call Centers, E-Commerce Driving Customer Loyalty", companies engaged in e-commerce should ensure that their call centers are in order before spending time and money on cutting edge e-commerce applications. The conclusion is that enterprises should rank e-commerce as their most important investment priority, but call center applications are ranked first in terms of functional importance. Ideal CRM occurs when old-fashioned call centers meet with state-of-the-art applications.

Hybrid businesses that combine brick-and-mortar call centers as well as internet CRM practices in a brick-and-click environment will thrive over the next three to five years. Technology must back the strategy. This is obvious, however, the emerging failure we are beginning to recognize from CRM is that even the best technology is useless when it is backed by the wrong strategies and enterprise priorities.

The Benefits of Technology

The ideal customer-enabled enterprise will be one that allows an enterprise to compile, share and view information gathered from every customer engagement—be it from the internet, the mail, the contact call center, face-to-face, or chat. The ideal "demand" engine is a single platform managing all media streams.

With every contact or call the enterprise terminates, it should immediately start playing messages, collecting digits, hitting databases and making very sophisticated routing decisions; skills based and call prioritization type routing. Blending of agent resources becomes extended to include not only inbound and outbound voice, but chat, shared browsing, and eventually, video. Monitoring applications are made easier in the single platform environment. Monitoring a chat session should be as effortless to set up as monitoring a voice call.

The strategic view to customer web based self service must include the essential—in fact crucial—perspective that customers must have easy access to appropriate information.

An example of web-based technology being used to personalize an online interaction is the capability for a live customer representative to speak, or chat, with the customer during the customer's online visit over an IP-based voice connection.

When considering enterprise technology investments, these can be better managed by selecting open architecture platforms and software tools that have the most flexibility to adapt to more complex market and customer demands.

Not all companies have all technologies yet. Investing in scalable, open technology enables the enterprise to fully integrate customer service solutions in the future based in part on email, chat, web call back, voice over IP, and ultimately, video. Open architecture is required because, as the nature and context of customer needs and preferences changes over time, companies must have the ability to insert or remove particular technologies as they see fit.

At a customer level, it becomes quickly apparent the advantage in how fast an enterprise can create services and applications. Speed to market is so crucial that companies cannot afford to have a period of adjustment in which they break in their new customer service solutions. They need complete solutions that can be implemented swiftly and efficiently while striving for seamlessly improving customer service. The speed at which companies enable bringing customer service applications to market is a key competitive differentiator.

Conclusion

The information age has brought intense customer focus. It is no coincidence that those companies that are consistently rated highly for their extensive customer relationships, reputations for superior customer service, and customer loyalty are the same companies that are using superior technology to deliver a consistent customer experience.

Enterprises that develop e-business leadership in their respective markets and industries will be the ones that are using state-of-the-art technology to establish new levels and standards of customer satisfaction. This is the only way in the 21st century to create and sustain a competitive advantage.

However, soon the benchmark of consistency will no longer be good enough. Customer engagements no longer need to be consistent, they need to be better. Eventually, consistent customer experiences become just that— consistent. Just as the "e" in "e-business" or "e-commerce" goes away, all business and all commerce is electronic.

Enterprises today cannot survive, much less succeed, in an increasingly more strategic world that requires a consistent customer experience regardless of the time, media or channel customers choose to use. Customers today expect the enterprise to be able to execute an engagement, a demand, across any channel. Anything less cannot be and is not, by definition, complete service.

There are two key elements required to fulfill the vision of comprehensive, competitive and sustainable customer interaction management. First, the company must have a consistent view of the customer across the enterprise regardless of media, channel, route or path. The view of the customer must include not only his history, but also analytical suppositions about the customer's future likelihood of buying. The majority of the CRM and ERP management solutions offered today accomplish this initiative.

The second requisite of customer interaction management is a comprehensive, stable and unified customer interaction system. If the enterprise's goal is a consistent customer experience, the benchmark of acceptable consistency should not be different, regardless of however the customer chooses to engage the enterprise—be it fax, voice, chat, email, video or mail.

Market forces today are being shaped by a new generation of customer. Power is shifting to the buyers from the sellers. A customers who is mobile, informed and device savvy. Customer interactions with the enterprise are more dynamic than ever. Technology is forcing a shift in the balance of power back to the technology and device-enabled consumer. Given the opportunity to traverse media, applications, and channels, customers will.

Competitive advantages are being won through the new array of channels, media, and devices. All of which customers will demand to use. Enterprises must maintain consistency over these channels. Those enterprises that have superior, multi-channel, customer-focused capabilities will succeed. Now, customers' loyalties may prevail and they may return later through some other channel, but from an enterprise perspective this may represent a failure for that one single engagement. Accumulate these experience failures and the consequences become obvious.

This strategic brief is intended to present a customer interaction philosophy that includes the idea that the foundation of enterprise success lies in the critical piece of customer interaction management. When the enterprise combines state-of-the-art technology with an intense focus on the customer demands and experiences, it will gain a long-term sustainable competitive advantage.

Successful enterprises that will strategically deploy and implement technology that enables understanding of how customer needs, preferences, and desires of those most profitable Pareto customers are changing over time. Success belongs to the enterprise that seizes the realization that the imperative is now in focusing on the customer demands in the form of the media that they, not in the enterprise, chosen to use.

21st century profits will be gained one customer at a time; one customer experience at a time. Today, customer demands, customer satisfaction and customer loyalty are gained engagement-by-engagement, media-by-media. Effectively managing the demands of customers requires efficiently managing the channels they choose to use. As enterprises retool for the information age, greater emphasis will be placed on the technology, interfaces, and media of this new demand generation.

The application of technology to serve customer focused strategies is essential to successfully managing customer interactions and relationships. The management of customer demands and their interactions in a way that creates consistent customer experiences is the only sustainable way to create a true competitive edge in the future.

Chapter Three
Another Typical Information Age Epiphany

Best Buy stores have been around as long as I have, since at least the early 60's. I have grown up going to Best Buy stores. It should be no surprise that I frequent my local Best Buy store for stuff such as CDs, film, cameras, boom boxes, batteries and other products and appliances I need from time to time. I am a stereotypical Best Buy customer, no pun intended.

Best Buy does one of the best jobs at CRM and practicing a "return on relationship" that I know of. I have to think that a big part of gaining a return on relationship is about just getting the customer to return, which I would personally know about in this case because I am a frequent Best Buy customer.

As a writer and speaker, I have a rule that I do not write or tell customer service stories about companies that I do not do business with myself. Like most of you, I have my own set of great customer service stories and bad customer service stories. Just recently, and mostly because I am researching the subject, I noticed that my local Best Buy was getting a much higher "return on relationship" from me than usual. My wife also noticed and whined that I was buying too many CDs and other electronic gadgets.

Until relatively recently though, my attention and loyalty were being persuaded by Best Buy's competitors. Sure, I was still loyal enough to stop by and check out the prices at a Best Buy, but I wasn't loyal enough that Best Buy was the only placed I stopped. Best Buy was regularly losing my attention fast, especially since the internet came along and gave me all sorts of information and options to buy more cheaply exactly what Best Buy was selling.

But I have noticed something funny happening at Best Buy recently; the things I was receiving in the mail started matching the things I wanted to buy. I got coupons for the CDs I actually was interested in and timely information on digital cameras that I was thinking about. Best Buy actually seemed to be giving more of a damn about who I was and what I wanted in a noticeable way.

It's a good thing, because the things that I am buying seem to be getting more complex and sophisticated all of the time. I am no dumb consumer. When you are buying a stereo component or a DVD player today, the customer knows enough to shop, not for just a piece of hardware, but also for the support the customer gets after he puts it in.

So, being relatively curious about the discriminating service I seemed to be getting from Best Buy and needing a great proof point to be in a book about customer service, I wanted to discover a little bit about why Best Buy was becoming branded as the better deal by millions of customers like me. Was Best Buy really caring that much more about me?

Another Typical Information Age Epiphany

Since its beginnings in the 1960's, every customer interaction with Best Buy was an anonymous one. Best Buy never knew the difference between their best customer and their worst customer, nor did they care. Best Buy never needed to care who they were.

Best Buy has traditionally been tightly partnered with mass marketing media such as newspapers. Getting new customers meant that all they had to do was run a bunch of ads in the local papers or run a fancy Sunday flyer, build a bunch of stores and people would come buy stuff. For most of this time, Best Buy's mission was to just push boxes out the front door. At the time, things like call centers, customer service and customer managed relationships were not really needed or relevant.

Best Buy really woke up and saw the light early in 1999 in terms of transforming themselves from a product-centric company to a customer-centric company. This was right about the time that I, and an entire generation of people, began to throw our hands up in the air over the growing complexity of consumer products. Now, an entire generation of internet educated consumers realizes the value in being able to actually go to a store and see what a $400 digital camera looks and feels like.

Best Buy's epiphany came when they realized that there was more value in understanding how many times customers came back than in how many boxes went out the door. When Best Buy realized that the information about the might be worth more than the transaction itself, they became a proof point of the evolution from the industrial age to the information one.

Bricks Drive Clicks

Best Buy is also a proof point for the idea that bricks drive clicks. At the end of this phase of dot com market e-xuberance, the successful e-commerce companies will likely be the successful retailing companies. It is the companies that have huge retail points of presence who, because they have the last mile—the connecting piece—will have an obvious competitive advantage over the pure dot com e-tailers that don't have brick and mortar stores.

It will be the Wal-Marts, the Home Depots, the Sam's Clubs, and the Best Buys of the world that ultimately prosper in the 21st century's customer charged economy. And just because these companies are late getting into the game does not mean they don't know how to play the game. From a consumer/customer standpoint, Best Buy seems to be evolving right along at the pace that I am.

It is easier to build clicks than it is to build bricks. Until dishwashers can come through DSL, Best Buy is likely to be what the final mile looks like for many of my retail needs, mostly because the cheapest way to deliver retail goods to people is still by mass distribution of trucks and cars. The use of semi trucks to deliver to a store and customers picking up their goods in their trucks and cars remains the most efficient way to transport things that fit in car trunks. Best Buy actually specializes in loading up the semi trailers full of appliances and making the rounds in my neighborhood. And it turns out that it is cheaper for Best Buy to do its own deliveries than it is to have UPS or FedEx do it for them.

Until Gateway, Dell and Amazon.com build out 400 stores, they won't have the solid brick infrastructure that it will take to profitably deliver consumer goods the final mile—at least not for the next several years. Besides, Best Buy has something that Amazon.com does not—Best Buy has a store within ten minutes of 80 percent of the US population.

And while Best Buy would admit that they are a little slow getting into the clickstream, the dot com companies are certainly moving pretty fast to get into bricks. Amazon.com, as an example, is looking more and more like a brick and mortar company every day. Gateway is building Country Stores everywhere. The dot coms are buying brick and mortar companies and already hold a tremendous amount of square feet of real estate themselves.

Information is Currency

In the world of complex devices, computers and appliances, Best Buy has insightfully realized that the information age has placed them squarely in the focus of directing, managing and channeling huge amounts of information flow. Best Buy has always managed the information flow of their markets from before the customer sale to after the sale, but never have they put the two together in any meaningful way. And when they did, the likely outcome was a little more useful than exhaust.

Best Buy is actually in the information business. The epiphany Best Buy had was a realization about taking the exhaustive flow of information that they were sitting in the middle of and turning it into a form of currency. Best Buy is embracing the idea that the juicy sweet spot of their future role in the retail food chain is as an infomediary, not as a retailer.

It should be no surprise that one of the most lucrative parts of Best Buy's business is in insurance, called Performance Service Plans. Insurance, it could be argued, is nearly a pure information business.

What does Best Buy do with the information that results from becoming so customer centric?

On a macro basis, Best Buy obviously does fairly sophisticated analysis and data mining on small market segments or even on the entire customer database. The information gleaned from this level drives the kinds of decisions around where to put stores and what general customer trends are. These are the kind of analytical things that marketing, merchandising and advertising people would work with.

However, it is on the micro basis, the one-to-one relationship with me the customer, that Best Buy has made the most useful changes.

Have you tried to buy a digital camera or a DVD player recently? Most consumers today anticipate a fair amount of complexity whenever they buy a digital camera or DVD, but most consumers would be shocked to discover that they now must actually program the new generation of washing machines. Unfortunately, like many of you, my VCR is still blinking 12:00.

I have never understood why the manufacturers of electronic devices could not build stuff that was easy to use. The sad fact is that appliances, devices, electronics, games and things with batteries in particular, have only gotten more complex and sophisticated. Best Buy realizes that a significant opportunity lies not only in being good at just retailing complex goods and appliances, but in being good at providing the information that goes along with these very complex products, appliances and devices. I think that they are dead on right.

This is where the internet has deeply affected Best Buy's future as they see it. After 40 years of experience, Best Buy still very much knows how to take care of the customers that come into their stores, but now Best Buy has realized that those customers have also got eyeballs. Best Buy believes that if they can take care of those eyeballs on the web, the chances are better that they are likely to be able to get the feet that belong to those eyeballs into their stores.

The information age epiphany is about realizing that the information about the products and services that they sell may be as important a part of the product as the product itself. Using the internet to provide and collect information is now a large part of the stickiness Best Buy believes that compels people to its stores.

The Best Buy web site does reflect an infomediary mission and purpose. For a consumer retail site, it has very deep contextual content. In my quest for information about digital cameras, Best Buy has the best. Thanks Best Buy. You just gained a small piece of my loyalty simply for organizing the sheer volume of information about the complex features digital cameras have today. You scratch my back; I'll scratch yours. And even though I am price conscious, I will likely even pay a little bit more in price at Best Buy for that camera.

Best Buy's customers are smart customers and Best Buy seems to like their customers that way. It may seem contrary, but educated customers, in the macro sense, do not cost Best Buy revenue. It might be easy to think that they would cost more because of longer and heavier interactions. Best Buy now clearly knows that in the long run, I am going to buy more. If Best Buy were smart, they would keep sending me emails about the 50 disc DVD carrousel changer for the 45 DVD discs they know I have purchased over the past nine months.

I don't think that Best Buy has underestimated what the internet has done to educate the typical consumer today. When considering complex electronic products today, people will use the internet to do their research and education about what they want to buy, particularly for information about extremely complex home theater and entertainment center configurations. Often customers know more about the products and services in a Best Buy store than the very people working there.

Another not so obvious facet to Best Buy's likely success in the digital age is the influence of the demand for convenience and speed from customers today. This is where the obviousness of Best Buy's bricks-drive-clicks strategy becomes neatly apparent. Why should I, as a digital camera customer, go to my northwest Houston neighborhood Best Buy store and pick it up? I don't want to wait five days and pay for two-day shipping.

If we can gain speed and efficiencies in drive-through fashion for hamburgers and Happy Meals, why can't we do it for digital cameras, batteries and CDs? Besides, it is a visceral part of human nature and instinct that we want to touch, see and look at the device or appliance we are buying—even CDs.

Best Buy has always been good at getting people in through the front door and they realize that eyeballs are just now becoming as important as feet. But it is the back door that Best Buy is paying particular attention to.

Because technology now allows us to keep track of each and every dialog we have with customers, Best Buy can keep track of detailed information about specific customers and their needs, preferences and desires as they evolve over time.

What Best Buy is doing with this information early on is using it in profiles that guide customers on what peripheral gear and equipment is recommended or will even work with existing components. The obvious advantage here is to make additional offers of peripherals to that customer. Best Buy knows that I, as a customer, come into a store and buy a couple of CDs or DVDs every month. Best Buy knows I obviously have a home audio. Best Buy wants to move me up the customer value chain by incentivizing me to buy something else.

If Best Buy would continue to show me the value in allowing me to know what kinds of products and services I have preferred or considered in the past, then they can really tailor some terrific specific reasons for me to keep coming back to them in the future. I don't think of Best Buy as a store for batteries and CDs, it's a place where I go to get smart recommendations for complex products.

Bricks and Clicks

As a futurist, I can easily foresee the day when Best Buy becomes so good at keeping track of the demands, needs and preferences of their customers as they are evolving over time, that they can instantly identify writers who mention them in great service stories and reward them with cash on the spot.

Best Buy is not a bleeding edge company—which is good because I, as a customer, do not want to be experimented on. What I want as a customer is technology that connects with me in meaningful ways that help me, not help them.

I am writing about Best Buy because they demonstrate a couple of proof points about how success will likely be found in the 21st century. Bricks drive clicks and information is a form of currency in the information age.

As a Best Buy customer, I am beginning to finally recognize the pragmatic consequences of applying technology to manage customer relationships. Best Buy is no dummy and neither are their customers. The demand to synergize the dot com world with the brick and mortar world cannot be denied in the 21st century. In the long run, which is the only run that matters, successful companies will be the ones that figure out how to build with the best of both. The best strategy is like the Best Buy strategy—

Chapter Four
E-Service and Healthcare

Any decent futurist can tell you what's next. The really good ones will tell you how fast what's next gets here. Today, the acceleration of the information age has left no sector turned-over or inside out. It is an amazing change happening when grandparents complain about the Baylor University Hospital nursery not getting newborn baby pictures on the web fast enough!

Don't mix the message with the metaphor. There will be nearly 65 million web-enabled grandparents by the year 2030, double what it is today. This mass aging will create a spectacular and brutal reformation in the way health care is provided in the Western world. Technology will be the platform and the internet will be the catalyst for this massive change. Health care in its spectrum of forms today, from provider to patient, will be unrecognizable in as little as seven to ten years. It will be the stunning acceleration, a supernova in the universe of health care that will catch most unawares. The entire food chain of the medical and health care spectrum will change.

[Factoid: Within four years electronic health care commerce will be $370 billion industry, 60 percent comprising insurance claims.]

There has been a core change in the beliefs about how people feel about health care and its providers. Technology will enable a new wave of empathy and care for illness, disease, and stress. It is important to advance on the ecology of the technology of health care from the patient perspective. This is from where the idea of "e-health" emerges.

E-health is the ecology of blending technology with medical care and knowledge. The internet profoundly represents the single most powerful change in patient care since the invention of the scalpel. Not only has the internet enabled the more open and free access to medical knowledge, it has fostered deeply stimulating and profound conversations and communications in a way that increases social health in general.

However, although today the internet is certainly more than just a prediction, its potential to transform health care remains untapped. Resistance, in the form of historical inertia, will continue to drag the viscosity of the e-health transformation. Health care's deeply embedded historical inertia means it has the greatest gulf to cross, the farthest to swim.

Every hospital, doctor, provider, and patient in the Western World is using "e-health". Examples of the "e-clinic" of e-health are here. Already, patients prick their fingers squeezing a drop of blood onto a glucose meter the size of a wallet, plug the meter into a PC, then after a few mouse clicks the patients sends the information (two weeks worth) to their doctors. This is the type of cyber-examine that happens daily at diabeteswell.com.

Technology is making it possible for doctors and nurses to collect data from patients on-line, then send back evaluations and instructions. The internet has emerged as the next to best medium for disseminating patient records and information, alerts and notifications, and a forum for current medical findings.

So why, if technology is so great, will e-health appear to move sluggishly toward the efficiencies, economies, and productivity technology has promised?

[Factoid: For the first time ever in September of 1999, visits to health related websites exceed those to adult content sites.]

That's the Hype, Here's Some Reality

In the race to connect doctors, patients, health plans, and pharmacies over the internet, health related enterprises are turning to an "e-health" based on the internet to tackle a number of challenges. The next generation of "e-health" exploits the convergence of several trends; the increasing consumer demands for health-related information, rising health care costs, the explosion of corporate intranets, and speedy advancements in web-based personalization technology.

The US health care industrial sector consumes $1.1 trillion annually, which is around 13.5 percent of the gross national product. More than $700 billion was spent on healthcare in the US alone in 1998. The economics of "e-health" are simple; it is getting bigger, not only faster. In a dubious demonstration of the immensity of dot com and internet technology in general, somebody obviously believes in the future of e-health as recently the two most competitive companies in the "e-heath" arena agreed to merge, a transaction valued at $5.4 billion.

Critical nurse shortages, sleep-deprived doctors, complex medical equipment, regulatory uncertainties, and costlier claims from an aging population needing doctors and hospitals more often than ever are driving up costs. The standards for optimal care are always changing. As a consequence, healthcare costs, after having remained steady for the past five years and showing a period of slower growth in the late 1990's, are rising fast again. Corporate health care costs alone will rise 8 to 10 percent this year.

Health care has become expensive, bureaucratic, and inconvenient. Health care has penetrated deeply into specialized segments, with specialized data derived from specialized systems. The sheer complexity of modern healthcare combines with systems that make it easy to make mistakes and create gross inefficiencies.

E-health, by any definition, requires changes to the core of problems that are endemic, systemic and ultimately terminal. For example, patient and consumer access to information can no longer be slowed or impeded by arrogant doctors and administrative bureaucrats. Often patients know more about their conditions than their treating physician.

Health care deals with the most complicated forms of self perpetuating forms of paperwork ever invented by man, based on budgets restricted by managed care and government bureaucracies. One of the most expensive challenges of e-health today, and one that will likely remain for some time, is paper and distribution costs. The maze of paperwork in a market valued at over $100 billion can be labyrinthine. Many estimate that the total annual amount of administrative waste in health care business is around $250 billion, that's almost $1,000 per person. Healtheon/WebMD estimates that $280 billion is spent on unnecessary administrative and clinical costs.

Digitizing health care makes sense, since it starts by reducing paper and transportation costs. The "e-health" industry has been racing to make healthcare more cost efficient by linking disparate, paper dependant parts and people such as doctors, patients, hospitals, pharmacies, labs, and insurance providers.

For all but the wealthy, healthcare has standards of service that would make any other enterprise get ill. And these are standards in any other market segment that customers would never tolerate. Many other industries have dramatically already proven the efficacy of web technology to reduce errors and increase productivity. The health care industry is currently at the slow end of the inertia scale, but shear historical momentum will make the changes to health care deep for certain, unpredictable at least, and spectacular at best.

[Factoid: The healthcare industry has grown to an estimated 30 billion annual transactions (the largest doing only 2 billion alone in the US per year, including claims submissions and patient referrals. Only 10 percent of these 30 billion transactions are now done electronically.]

Digital Deaths

We don't have to all climb high mountains or sit for long times in cold caves to realize the tremendous medical benefits of technology. Technology saves lives; perhaps it will even save yours someday. From a pure economic perspective we can point to the fourth leading cause of death in this country, medical errors, as an immediate application point for he pragmatic use of medical technology.

Medical mistakes and unintended, but avoidable consequences, kill somewhere between 44,000 and 98,000 hospitalized Americans each year. President Clinton recently called for simpler technology to minimize medical errors. Physician handwriting needs to be eliminated from the equation and computer transmission is the obvious answer.

For a $30 million investment, Veterans Administration hospitals tag patients with barcodes to ensure they swallow the right medicines. A computerized cart pulls in to the patients room, scans the patient's barcode bracelet, and out pops the appropriate medication Joe is scheduled to take that hour. Alarms notify the nurse when the wrong pill or dosage is about to be delivered. Medication errors have dropped 64.5 percent since the VA Hospital in Topeka KS introduced bar codes.

Sometimes drugs with similar names get mixed up or the pharmacy supplies the wrong information on how to take the medicine, when, with or without food, and what to do if you miss a dose. When patients are prescribed drugs, they need to know the correct dosage, what it treats, what it interacts with, and what are the known side effects. Counting the brand name and generic varieties of prescription medicines, there are almost 10,000 to choose from all with known and unknown side effects when combined with any other compound.

The advent of big bandwidth wireless now means that technology can enable us to get exact instructions, treatments, and protocols at the point of treatment. In major hospitals many doctors are increasingly prescribing drugs and treatments via computer, hand held PalmPilots and similar devices. These computerized prescription pads eliminate the interpretation of doctor's notoriously bad handwriting and the computer double checks patient charts for safe drug matching—avoiding the patient being given the wrong medical procedure, medication, or even dosage. Incorrect diagnosis or delays in treatments can be reduced as well.

Bureaucracy affects e-health as well. Out of the tens of thousands of compounds that are discovered each year, only 7 percent of them make it into your drug store. Delays in the regulatory approval cycle can cost a pharmaceutical firm upwards to a million dollars a day or more. Health care companies are required to provide enormous amounts of critical data throughout the long, complex, and expensive drug testing trials and cycles.

The FDA review process requires literally mountains of paper, one million pages on average. One million pages is roughly a tractor-trailer full of paper and could have as many as 20,000 page sections, with which reviewers had to read through stacks 5 to 6 feet in depth. The typical review process takes 18 to 24. In an effort to move this documentation through the FDA's approval process, "e-health" has been influenced by the emerging electronic-based drug submission process. Pfizer cut that 24 months down to 12 without compromising safety. Eliminating the centuries old, paper-centric way of submitting documentation to the FDA, gave the company the ability to deliver five new drugs every 12 months, leading the industry.

The use of technology will prevent medical mistakes. As an example, when choosing a hospital make sure to ask if they have a computerized drug system where prescriptions are checked against patient records for allergies, or other risks. Such systems are proven to reduce errors.

E-health and Health Prevention

[Factoid: Online prescription sales will reach $1 billion by 2002, compared with $33 million in 1999.]

Companies realize that employee wellness is in their economic self-interest. Providers of health care also realize that patient wellness is in their economic self-interest. There is tremendous savings, and health, to be had when you move people from exponentially expensive high-risk categories to medium and low risk categories. Humana is a company, for example, specifically focused on realizing significant savings from keeping better track of those ten percent of their patients who account for 80 percent of the costs. When you can identify them, you can monitor them and when patients comply with treatment and protocols, they stay healthier and cost less.

The internet is at last making it possible to collect and manipulate every discrete piece of provider information to patient data—information such as visitation histories, lab reports, x-rays, prescriptions, appointments and scheduling, purchasing, and insurance claims. Then throw in the availability of your complete drug, vitamin, diet, and supplement history, including all prescription medications, over the counter drugs, and dietary needs.

Emergence of Health Information.

The internet now provides an infrastructure to implement rudimentary "e-health" plans. Dozens of portals, communities, and advice web sites contend for consumers hungry for healthcare information. E-health is certainly something much deeper than a flurry of dot com campaigns on everything from Fox News Reports, talk-radio, billboards and CVS pharmacy bags. In spite of the 15,000 healthcare "content" sites today, patients seek more from the internet than just more information. Most of all of the "e-health" content sites today are quickly evolving into "e-health" portals.

Some 70 million people searched the web for healthcare information in 1999. As of 2/2000, the internet supported an estimated 15,000 health related sites. Most of e-health's marketing pitch is focused on prevention. The web's biggest information site, WebMD's OnHealth has more than 7 million members. In recent months, there have been some 3.8 million visitors to WebMD's website. Staywell.com, mydailyhealth.com, and Mayo Clinic's Healthquest are all closed intranet or extra-net offerings marketed to employers and health insurers who buy access for constituents.

This cyber population seeks wellness and health information, sharing that information in on-line support groups and communities. E-health is about a new type of employee benefit one tailored to the hyper-stressed gold collar worker. Websites offer advice from posture and nutrition to on-line consultations with medical experts.

On-line medical monitoring companies such as LifeMasters and Health Hero already provided disease management services. Through opt-in registration and monitoring site visits, one e-health company generates data for customizing and personalizing promotions and treatments. One already proven method is through free newsletters and other consistent, current, health related issues.

Many major healthcare content sites are swiftly reducing their dependence on advertising by adding on-line pharmacies, medical claims processing, and other innovative services. The emerging markets will be in the software applications built around becoming consumer on-line medical managers.

Web sites have already given patients access to vast amounts of reference material. Armed with facts, and sometimes armed without them, net savvy patients are taking increasing responsibility for their conditions. New medical findings change weekly and doctors have little time to keep up.

The internet is creating a form of evidenced-based medicine because it enables conscientious use of the most up-to-date information and technology for making decisions about health care. Internet customers are demanding better health as a consequence of the better information available. In this day of the internet knowldege-ified patient, they can know more about their condition and treatment options than the doctors they talk to.

The internet, for example, provides current medical research on thousands of specific medical conditions. For evidenced based health care to work this requires doctors and practitioners to have access to health care information near where they work with their patients. Bringing information closer to the point of treatment, means better service. This is where we will see the impact of wireless in health care—information, anytime, anywhere.

It is in the managing of the complex tangle of relationships, regulations, and technology that will characterize the health care environment of tomorrow. Large e-health companies like Healtheon/WebMD are expecting to gain patient and customer loyalty by efficiently connecting them to their doctors, health plans, and pharmacies.

The Paradox of Progress Physician, e-Heal Thyself

It should come as no surprise that the best example for the resistance to change can be found at the very core of the health care profession, with physicians themselves.

No one disagrees about the tremendous advantages that laser scalpels have over metal blades. Today, only 6 percent of doctors use laser scalpels in spite of the health advantages—no bleeding, wound is cauterized, less infection, no sterilization, and so on. Incredibly, this figure has not changed for the past twelve years. Why? In a classic example of the paradox of progress, here is why. Given the choice to have major invasive surgery done on yourself, would you prefer a young medical school graduate with six years of experience with a laser scalpel operate on you, or a physician that has been using a razor for thirty-five years?

Forrester recently released a report titled, "Why Doctors Hate the Net." It says that not enough internet-based vendors understand the pressure on physician's time and that until doctors demand new technology, the providers will avoid the internet until the benefits are clear. Doctors are intimidated by the automating and putting on-line complex set of rules, algorithms that govern managed care, dictate treatments and prescribe the drugs patients require. Commonly today when a physician writes a prescription on their Palm Pilot VII and transmits, algorithms determine if the drug is medically safe, whether the health plan requires a different drug (or if additional approval is needed to prescribe the medication.

"E-health" faces big challenges. One is getting doctors to use the internet more. A survey by FIND/SVP/Cyber Dialogue revealed that 77 percent of patients prefer to get online healthcare information directly from their physicians, but just ten percent of doctors have a web page and give out their email addresses.

The early influence is the strongest. Healtheon currently stands as the colossus of the "e-health" industry. The fact that Healtheon/WebMD now has access to almost 90 percent of practicing physician's desktops, currently gives credence to the accusations of Microsoft-esque dominance of on-line healthcare. However, currently few of the subscribing physicians use the company's limited offering of services. Healtheon/WebMD, the largest "e-health" company, claims "relationships" with only 400,000 doctors and of that many it is clear that few actually use any of the on-line services.

Several companies are attempting to "re-intermediate" doctors and improve care by linking patients with their physicians online. Soon doctors will be able to access their office-based computer systems from home or other remote locations through an internet portal. Once a patient has been diagnosed, the physician electronically prescribes and emails appropriate information from his site to the patient. The end mission is that doctors will be able to access hospital and patient information from anyplace that they have internet access. For this to happen doctors will need to trust the system and hospitals need to stop being reluctant to introduce anything doctors have not embraced wholeheartedly.

E-Regulations

Health care in its current internet form is in sick and bad shape. "E-health" is getting off to a bad start as eroding consumer and patient trust inevitably deepens as a result of additional regulatory and uncertain legislative conduct. Today, e-health like internet taxation is beginning to get a little Washington's attention. However in an election, little more than hearings on cyberpharmacies will be done.

Heath-care web sites hope that self-regulation will succeed before the federal government gets involved. A broad coalition of industry players is trying to make things better before trouble with regulatory, civil and privacy issues starts. Twenty health related sites including AmericasDoctor.com, Drkoop.com, Mediconsult.com, and PlanetRx.com, and others, are working to agree on a fundamental set of ethics for the on-line medical information industry.

Until privacy, security and the credibility of digital signatures are addressed, regulatory influenced uncertainties mean new laws. Some will be impossibly burdensome. Many consumers will continue to fear environments with pervasive online privacy rights violations. A study released in February 2000 by the California Health Care Foundation (www.chcf.com), found 21 of the leading health sites provided very poor consumer privacy.

This study bashed all of the major sites for not delivering on privacy promises.

Getting consumers to trust a health site for medical information is one thing, persuading them to trust their health care with an on-line company is another. The federal government does have a genuine interest in spotting spikes in the sales of anti-diarrhea medicines at local pharmacies as an indication of water-supply contamination.

The Health Care Financing Administration, the federal agency that oversees Medicare and Medicaid is currently developing the most sweeping reforms in health care since the invention of the telephone. The biggest consequence will be a massive change in the transmission, portability, and storage of medical information. HIPAA compliance creates big opportunities for vendors and integrators, since virtually every health care provider will eventually have to reassemble their information infrastructure from the ground up.

The Technology of E-Health

Health care providers spent nearly $20 billion in 1999 on IT systems and services. Recent surveys suggest that more than 40 percent of the health care executives that responded said that they planned to upgrade their networks and infrastructures during the next twelve months. The survey also discovered that 91% of these companies are using their web sites for promotion and marketing, 71% for employee recruitment, 60% for communication with physicians, 58% for consumer health information, and 75% for online physician and provider referral and directories.

"E-health" also faces a challenge shifting older proprietary networks to an IP based internet—one where doctors and patients can access them more easily. Many enterprises, particularly hospitals, will need to upgrade their networks because their existing infrastructure cannot handle increasing amounts of traffic. From a pure technology perspective, networks will be the single largest investment that health related enterprises will make over the next several years.

More healthcare organizations are turning to outsourcing as they realize that information technology is not their core competency. Health care providers look to off-load routine IT operations and to focus on more strategic IT projects such as electronic business. In some hospital environments standards on the quality of service of its computing systems are approaching telephony grade. Industry help desk call times are among the call centers lowest. On-line systems consistently have 98 percent or better uptime.

To do this, most health care enterprises will have to spend between $300,000 and $1 million to create an internet presence beyond corporate brochure-ware. Compared to relative older technologies such as telephony or accounting, most health care enterprises are mostly for promotion or recruiting services.

Some 185,000 doctors nationwide use a form of medical practice management software applications to manage their practices. Automating the intricacies of insurance, the nuances of eligibility, physician selection and preferences, claim status and records, verification creates efficiencies that even the most technologically challenge physician can see.

E-health is an E-mess

One of the responsibilities of a futurist is to make sure that decisions are not made in denial—denials about trends, applications, demographics, and the fact that the US healthcare system is chronically ailing. The hype about the pace of change far exceeds the true pace of change.

The entire chain, from provider to physician to patient, wants to believe that the internet and "e-health" will change people's lives for the better, forever. This is a shared mass vision of billions of digitally glazed eyeballs where the internet is the technological catalyst for revolutionizing health care—a vision where hundreds of millions of people go get health information, schedule appointments with their physicians, request prescription refills, review medical records, and transact all kinds of the other information. The vision is that doctors will sign on to communicate with patients, file claims, get lab results, write prescriptions, schedule appointment, and order supplies.

However, a sweeping perspective of all industrial technologies shows that there exists a consistent phenomena in health care that exists in every information based industry. That is that the pragmatic application of technology isn't near as common as the demonstrable use of technology. Doctors, and patients in particular, are skeptical because they know claims processing systems have not improved from the consumer's perspective. For example, tele-medicine has been technically feasible for some time, but it is still not very widespread.

E-health's progress is likely to remain slow mostly due to the massive historical inertia of health care in general. Physicians struggling to contend with managed care do not want to take on any more responsibility. Medical equipment manufactures continue to be reluctant to wire their devices to the net until doctors and patients demand the capability. A net that many doctors are resisting anyway.

Health care's most pressing problem is the communication, or lack of, between patients and doctors. One of the challenges of "e-health" is the risk that messages often get mixed up. It is still confusing when patients think a website is for doctors and doctors assume that it is meant for patients. Today, only a small minority of people is actually using on-line e-health services, but its usage is now larger than the adult content industry.

E-health's acceptance means that internet sites must be both ubiquitous and useful. Patients don't understand why their banks can go online, but their doctors can't.

Interactive health care still has many cultural, legal and technology hurdles to leap before nearing mainstream. Pure e-health internet plays such as drkoop.com are nearing the end of their life spans, suffering from the agony of now realizing that revenue is much more than a distraction.

E-health itself has many issues and barriers to the pragmatic application of technology—privacy and confidentiality, disclosure, e-commerce, content, and services. Specifically, the issue of the on-line practice of medicine is boiling to the forefront. Economic issues exist with current liabilities and the lack of direct revenue from health care sites.

Economic, regulatory, competitive, and clinical imperatives will help push interactive care through these barriers.

Shifting the use of "e-health" services and transactions to the low-cost internet, is inevitable because of one factor, cost. The complications from chronic diseases cost insurers billions annually. High tech medical monitoring and email combine to enable the gathering of ultra detailed records and revive the idea of the house call in digital form. More frequent patient updates means heading off complications before they happen.

The costs of e-health will come down over time because a more uniform system of health information will save the entire provider to patient food chain from having to deal with the gross inefficiencies and cost burdens that health care has been built on. Wiring up doctors, hospitals and pharmacies, insurers and clinics should make the administration of health care more efficient and convenient for consumers. Easy on-line access to medical information should help people educate themselves and take more responsibility and control over their own health. Remote monitoring and broadband video should give people in rural areas access to care once available only in cities.

There is no industry segment more suited for technology-based improvement than that of healthcare. The challenge will be to produce something socially beneficial rather than just another way to shop. If "e-health" does become just another way to shop, then the entire "e-health" care sector will be discredited, compelling a longer acceptance cycle. The actual uptake of "e-health" may in fact be a bit slower than the hype.

Like many other business sectors today, media hype far exceeds the true pace of change. E-health is still in its clinical trial stage. The health information sites available today are but a small sampling of how technology will improve health care.

New business-to-business health related web sites capitalize on the tremendous popularity of consumer health sites. We are in fact moving generational-ly from just retrieving information off of the internet to specific tailored information for the patient's specific medical needs. In particular, large healthcare portals will build, buy, or align with care sites to offer a full range of care services that consumers demand.

Health care's problems were meant to be solved by the internet and the ultimate near perfect convergence is only a matter of time. It's happening already, some ten percent of the radiology images generated at Massachusetts General now travel over their network at some point. Real revolution will not happen with "e-health" until doctors and patients interact over the internet—when the health chart on your doctor's site is book-marked just like your sports, stock, and news pages.

E-health based and internet delivered health care will never substitute for personal physical care, but it does offer tremendous potential to eliminate in the 21st century, the tools we used in the 20th century·

Chapter Five
The Future is Calling

Eventually The Future Shows Up Everywhere

The most precious commodity of any writer is that of word count and I want to use some of up it up on a caveat emptor before we start on this article about the future of call centers and customer service. Being an industry futurist (perhaps this industry's only futurist) can be a tough mantle to wear, since anyone can do it. But I have to warn you that forecasting is difficult, especially about the future. Futurist Freeman Dyson said that, when it comes to useful futurists, it is better to be wrong than to be vague. So at the greater risk of being wrong, I'll take my best stab at not being vague.

To that end, I believe that the job of a good futurist is to make sure that readers and clients, you, don't make decisions in denial. Denials about the trends, demographics, and the influence of technologies that are seemingly unrelated to the business we are all in but never the less have a huge impact.

A final note on the business of futurism: there is an old African Proverb that says, "If you know your history, the future will not trouble you." And while you may be expecting me to talk about what's next, I think that the right place to start would be by discussing the very understated amount of persistent historical irony that defines the way we do the many things that we do. I refer to this as the Rosenberg Effect, after consultant and writer Art Rosenberg, who will be introduced in a later column, but whom could certainly tell a story or two about the depth of historical irony found in call centers.

The Rosenberg Effect

In web years, the new pace of the game, the technology of customer service, is old stuff. At more than 25 years now since the first ACD, we are almost ancient even. I often use the history of the standard railroad gauge and Erlang as examples of a pervasive Pavlov's conditioning that has occurred in our industry since it's beginning.

At four feet eight and one-half inches from track to track, today's standard railroad gauge is a two horse-butts evolutionary vestige of the width of war chariot wheel ruts carved in roads all over Northern Europe by the Roman Imperial army. Ironically, today we have the very fiber optic lanes of the information superhighway built into the very railroad beds and snaked through the pipeline right of way's that built the industrial revolution.

Erlang, the very statistical tool so many enormously depend on today was ultimately based on the statistical algorithms used by Napoleon to determine how many artillery and cannon balls were needed to lob into the opposing forces for the maximum number of kills. How many trunks needed to answer callers is a derivative of how many cannons were necessary to kill troops in enemy formations. Sometimes, with the way I get treated as a customer, I wonder if the same "kill the enemy" mentality exists: how appropriate.

Here is another interesting historical irony more closely related to our industry. When we go back and examine the birth dates of every major communications devices over the past 150 years, an interesting pattern appears. Starting with the telegraph (in railroad right of ways), then telephone, radio, television, first networked computer (qwertyuiop was the first e-mail message) and to when PCs with modems outsold those without, we find the emergence of a major consumer communication device roughly every 30 years or so. So, according to that hypothesis, we should have some fifteen years still to go before the next.

It is contra to human nature to adopt new interfaces and devices quite as quickly as the popular media would have us believe. Our culture is pragmatic on whole and we don't change our interface quite so easily. The fact that we are growing older demographically further contributes to the pace of technology adoption. Everyone says it, but when was the last time you actually "dialed" a telephone?

Even the Y2K bug itself is the epitome of a persistent vestige of history. Y2K is an evolutionary self- perpetuated phenomena that came about, not as a consequence of lack of disk space or limitations on it's precursor punch cards, but from the early accounting ledgers on which programming was written. By the way, the first computers were simply calculators used to calculate, guess what, the trajectories of artillery shells. There is a certain kind of comedic fatality in the Y2K issue, as I believe that the apocalyptic hype and paranoia has indeed served a very useful purpose. This isn't my term, but it is appropriate to call Y2K at this point, digital Darwinism, where all the right clocks are going to get cleaned, no pun intended.

If you don't know your history, you may be surprised to discover that the world's oldest profession has a lot to do with our industry. Oh yes, you see the world's oldest profession is also the world's oldest form of customer service. The fact remains that when we go back and look at the emergence of most every impactful medium starting with movies, the Polaroid camera, the 8mm film, and the VHS video format (which emerged because superior PAL format wasn't allowed to be licensed for adult content videos), we see another proof point for the acceptance and adoption of most every major communications technology.

The internet today is a medium where an estimated 25 – 60 percent of all traffic, by bandwidth, is devoted to adult content sites. It was only in September of this year that on-line traffic to health related sites surpassed on-line traffic to adult content sites for the first time. Early adopter experiences with credit card transactions, voice over IP, video, chat, security, authentication, customer profiling and data mining have come from the compelling economic engine built around adult content. The good news is that we are growing out of this fairly rapidly as our culture can handle only so much porn and bomb-building instructions. We will grow out of it larger, which is different than faster, than anyone could have ever imagined.

In 1978 Ken Olsen told the World Future Society that there is no reason why anyone in the world would want a computer in his or her home. Yea, well, I really think that those Romans would be surprised to find that the width of two horse-butts still means something today. This is what I call evolutionary irony.

Historically, now that we have enough history to be historical with, we know that each generation of computers, devices, and interfaces do not force the previous one into extinction; no they actually have increased the demand for it. Each generation of technology and applications becomes an information supply source for the next, an existing base on which to exploit the capabilities of the newer generation of infrastructure and devices. Evolution proves that new technologies must wait for preceding ones to die out. Some, such as the width of chariot wheels and telephones, are enduringly persistent.

It's About Time

The most influential element of customer relationships in the future will be that of time. You see, as customers ourselves today, substituting activity for achievement is our biggest fear and time is fast becoming our most precious commodity. Your time, my time, our customers time, at every customer engagement do you ask yourself, as futurist George Gilder asks, if "you are a life-span extender or life-span vendor?"

In Fort Worth recently the post office removed the clocks behind the service counters that count off the days, hours, minutes and seconds to the year 2000 in big red numbers because they were a source of complaints. They were removed when they were linked to a decline in customer satisfaction surveys. It is increasingly bothering people to see, or hear (on hold), their lives counted away right in front of them.

But to the very customers that demand we do a better job of servicing them, time has a funny elasticity to it. A high-rise apartment building in Chicago had notorious slow elevators and ultimately the slow elevator reputation affected the value of the property. The expensive option was to install new million dollar elevators. The inexpensive alternative, installing mirrors on each of the floors, proved to be the solution as now customers had something to do—combing hair, adjusting ties, and checking for spinach in their teeth. Complaints plummeted. Same elevators, but because customers now had something distracting to do, the value of their time changed. We can apply this learning to call centers. We know that callers who are told how long their expected wait time will be would wait twice as long to abandon the call than those that weren't.

Managing and manipulating time is, after all, at the core what we are really good at in call centers. However, I suspect that what we are really good at in this industry is getting halfway faster to the wrong place we need to be going anyway. It is now a world where the batch-mode tools that we use to drill down into various aspects of last weeks business are increasingly becoming irrelevant.

Speed records are almost always broken by people with no place in particular to go. And while the C-level (CEO, CIO, CFO C-etc.) in our companies is being media-cized to think about the lifetime values of customers, to them, average talk time seems to be a trivial irrelevancy. What is important about the concept of CRM, and I am going to talk about the fallacies of CRM in a moment, is that it often contradicts the very efficiencies we strive to achieve in call centers. In this age of customer relationships, we want agents to talk longer to customers and philosophically, the concept of CRM is not about how fast we can react, it is about how far out we can think.

The future of call centers has a lot to do with understanding that it is the dialogs with customers where the new currency of the information age is being minted.

Infocentricity

There is a big three banking corporation that identified a precise date, November of 1998, when the value of the PC's sitting on their employees desktops in downtown Manhattan would be worth more than the value of the square foot of real estate the PCs occupied. Thirteen months later they identified an exact date when the value of the information in the PCs would be worth more than either the value of the PCs or the square feet of real estate they sat on.

If there ever was proof of the shift from the industrial age to the information age, this is it. One thing is for certain, technology is not where the power is; true power, which you may be calling revenues, profits or service levels, lies in the information that technology can generate. Information and knowledge are the currency of the information age. To demonstrate the new relative value of information, wouldn't you like to know to what web sites America's 3rd wealthiest man, Warren Buffet, is surfing too? In theory, Warren Buffet's ISP should know.

Call centers are exquisite knowledge sources and, as such, they are revenue sources. You see, the information age and info-centricity makes obsolete the contrast of calling call centers cost centers or profit centers. Call centers are information engines, and that makes them revenue engines.

Call centers are a proof point of the arrival of the generation of info-centricity. Info-centricity is about the move from product thinking to information thinking. I believe that the future of call centers is concentrated around the singular idea that there is only one true and pure source of raw customer information and that is at the point of engagement (human or machine) with the customer, the dialogue.

CRM Customer Relationship Manipulation?

It appears as though the immediate future of call centers seems quite packed with the ideas of CRM, Customer Relationship Management.

A recent Deloitte & Touche study reported that manufacturers can generate 60 percent more profit if they become customer centered. This is one of many emerging statistics that enterprise C-levels read in their Harvard Business Review's and Booz Allen's Business and Strategies magazines. These statistics are fueling the white-hot growing interest in call centers by the C-level.

But, for the most part wouldn't we agree that CRM is just another acronym for the same thing we have been doing in call centers all along? Isn't CRM just another name for customer care? Doesn't it mean avoiding having a disgusted customer on your hands because they call into your call center today about the email they sent yesterday and the agent has no access to it?

CRM is an executive-ized term for something we have always been doing, only speed is picking up. It has the silky allure of a successful buzzword being over-used by vendors, and more specifically consultants, to rise above market noise. Two years ago, at one of our industry's trade shows there was Call Center Live, this year at the same show it was CRM live, next year it will be ERM Live. After that it will be xRM. Being educated about CRM is different than being propagandized. Don't be distracted by the propaganda.

My definition of CRM is rooted in making a distinction between understanding who customers are and what they want. Isn't this what ANI, IVR, and screen popping are all about? Customer demands are different than their identities. Customers want to believe that you really want to know what they want, but our technology today is all about really needing to know who they are so you can screen pop and increase the transaction efficiencies we so maniacally desperately seek.

CRM is the difference between American Express instantly knowing who I am every time I call, and figuring out that, even though I eat out in a different city every week, I have never charged my airline tickets to those very cities. Certainly AMEX calls me often enough for some affinity marketing offer, but calling me to ask me how to increase my loyalty seems beyond them today.

As a final thought on CRM, your interpretation of it must be inclusive of the realization that loyalty is different than no choice and that eyeballs are not customers.

So, let's shift gears here and let's talk about the future. In particular I want to share with you my thoughts on what technology is going to have the most significant influence and impact on call centers over the next five years, and I am not talking about the internet.

Wicked Wireless Widgets

Hairs could be split over which statistics you could believe, but according to some the wireless technology of cell phones and PCS is actually growing faster than the internet. Today, there are some 83 million wireless subscribers growing at nearly 45,000 new subscribers per day in

North America. This is compared to the internets growth of 18,000 American households per day. Wireless phones are expected to reach 50% penetration by year 2002. Finland already has 106 percent penetration.

While the internet is a medium whose growth is driven almost entirely by the demand for knowledge, the growth of wireless phones is driven by a more powerful motivator, that of saving time. Contrary to the digitally heady internet pundits, I don't think that we are entering the age of the internet—no, we are emerging into the age of the wireless pervasive device and when Nokia, PalmPilot, and Siemens get together you know that whatever they are up to is something ubiquitous.

Keep your eye, perhaps better said your ears, on the intelligent edge. These portable wireless devices are proliferating fast, and they, not PCs, are blurring the boundaries between computers and communication. The impact of these new crop of intelligent devices are where call centers need to really be focused on. This is where customer evolution is really happening and the pervasive device is a proof point. Wireless devices should be high on the inventory of indices used to triangulate in on what's next. Pay close attention to the devices your customers use.

Webify or Die!

Today, in a world where the message is "webify or die," what works in the future would not be complete without comments on the impact of the internet. Let's face it, the internet is no longer just a prediction as we are solidly now a culture of the net-set and the world increasingly belongs to those that can skip from site to site with the ease of a speeding gazelle.

But the fact is that the internet has done little to relieve the congestion of calls into call centers today. The proliferation of web sites is actually creating an explosion of calls. Compounding the problem is the fact that what the internet has enabled customers that are often more knowledgeable about your company's products and services than the very agents to whom they talk. The internet creates knowledge-ified customers (accurately or not) and this increasingly leaves agents haplessly in the position of being "only authorized to apologize," as an agent with CompuServe told me recently.

For pragmatic purposes, the internet is a media fed frenzy about digitally glazed eyeballs living off of wild assumptions of 1000 percent compound growth rates every several months. Now, I am not that good at the math, but it does not take much to figure out that this growth is actually faster than growth of the very chips in the routers on which the net is built (Moore's Law). Besides, at compound growth rates like that, if you are off by a single degree you miss by thousands of miles. You can comfortably temper the hype with a rather large grain of salt.

The internet is facing its own kind of convergence (where has that buzz word been lately?) as relentless as telephony. Customers ultimately want real service, not something virtual. They want real products, not something virtual. Little known about virtual bookseller Amazon.com is that they now own more than 4 million square feet of very solid warehouse space. Internet start-up grocer Webvan is spending one billion dollars to build twenty-six 300,000 square foot warehouses over the next two years. Ask Jeff Bezos, CEO of Amazon.com, what the most important part of his business is and he will tell you that it is their call centers. You see, Amazon knows that one unhappy customer wont just tell 6, 10 or 25 other people, on the internet they will tell 6000.

Today, and I believe for some time to come, your enterprise's real competition will remain the telephone. If your company's web site cannot get customers to put down the telephone, then that web site is a poor substitute for the level of service a customer can get from picking up the phone. For now, there is no culturally embedded reflex in using the web for service. There is, however, a deeply ingrained cultural reflex to pick up the phone.

Letting Go of Our Erlangs

Other than perhaps the space shuttle and surgical equipment, no other technology discipline can claim greater reliability and consistency than that found in call centers. But this is a double-edged sword as call centers are where culturally rooted expectations about service levels have been set. Consumers will not retreat to inferior mediums as the failure of less-than-TV quality video has proven.

Call centers are an intellika, which is Latin for that point that exists between potentiality and actuality. Call centers are a proof point for the pragmatic application and adoption of technology. If it is not being used in a call center, it is not yet a real technology. IP telephony is an example. How many of you here are actually using IP telephony for customer service, not experimenting, not thinking about it, but actually using it?

Call centers are blessed because the future is fairly binary. It is either evolution or extinction. Our challenge today is how do we change a culture weighted down by its own historical inertia because, after 25 years, change can be tough for our industry because there is so much of it to change. Evolution requires an understanding of what causes extinction. From call centers to customer relationship management, success lies in understanding our history. There is plenty of it and that we are clearly, in a cynical sense, myopic sober slaves to old ways of doing things. I characterized this as "paving the cow-path" in one of my early books on call centers.

The new rules are that there are no rules. Be leery of self-perpetuating internet-based acronym driven buzzword traps such as CRM because aggregating eyeballs and increasing stickiness are often just slogans masquerading as strategy.

We must attach a different value to our customers and understand the C-level's perception of what time is and its value. It is no longer about speed of answer; it is about depth of relationships. Never ask me the same thing twice and don't waste my time not knowing who I am or how I plan to pay, let's get this transaction over with and I will call you back - sooner.

Call centers are a pure proof point for info-centricity. Positioned correctly and confidently, we do indeed generate the true currency, the big bills, of the information age. Bank on it, because your C-level will be WHAT if they have not already.

While the internet is capturing the hype, the hits will be coming from the telephone for some time to come. The Negroponte Switch (that which comes over the wire will be wireless (telephones) and that which comes over the air will come over the wire (cable TV)) is happening; voice is wireless and pervasive now. Keep in mind that customers were born with vocal chords and ears, not qwerty keyboards plugged into their heads.

The future? The future in our industry actually has little to do with technology. I believe that advances in technology are always driven by something else. In 1997 there were some 35 million drill bits sold in America. People don't want, and have never bought drill bits; what they want are the holes. We are in an industry that is full of experts about drill bits and looking at holes, which is what CRM is becoming, is something we will have to master in order to evolve. Can we let go of our Erlangs?

The ultimate proof point for the future of our industry lies with us, the human-ware, from C-level to cubical level. We must hire, work for, and be people who are going to live in the future that you the reader, not me, the writer/futurist, not the vendors, not consultants, not TeleProfessional Magazine, but the one you create. REWORD This will require acknowledging that not everything that worked in the past will work in the future. Can you really let go of those Erlangs?

And the future customer? This emerging generation of customers has a whole new set of behaviors that our current technologies cannot respond to. This is an internet-powered generation devoid of segmentation by age.

This demand generation has not adopted the internet; no, they have internalized it. This is the knowledge-ified demand generation and these customers want comprehensive and accurate information, plenty of choices, competitive prices and no-strings gimmicks. They do view their personal data as valuable and they expect you to as well. The demand generation is being raised on email and they don't necessarily need friendly face-to-face service although voice will remain their default medium for some time to come.

Future success in our business comes when you realize that we are no longer in the business of implementing technology and managing people. We are in the business of implementing change. Prepare for the future of the ever perpetual change because it is no longer about cost justification, it is about change justification. Can we let go of our Erlangs?

Chapter Six
The Future of Computer Telephony Integration

There are two meta-trends influencing the future of computer telephony. The first is the evolution of information as a form of currency where information about transactions becomes more valuable than the transactions themselves. This is also a part of the shift from transactional efficiencies to customer intimacies. The applications and technology of computer telephony will move away from the efficiencies of transactions as measured by Erlangs to the return on relationships currently represented by CRM. CT will evolve from being efficiency-oriented technology and applications to supporting experience-oriented applications.

The market potential for CT application is still huge, as only an estimated 30 to 42 percent of companies have implemented CTI applications other than screen popping. The burden of the industry is the effect of media-zation, the growing awareness at the technology level of the gap between vendor push and customer pull. This can be seen, for example, in the marketing of internet telephony and the actual implementations.

The second trend is the decentralization of customers, companies, and employees. The change of the endpoints is merging in the decline of the PC and the advent of the wireless devices and networks. Large enterprises will become conglomerations of regional branch offices and remote workers. Supported by the number of US internet users who employ mobile environments, wireless data will grow to be 78 percent of all mobile traffic within 18 months. This traffic is spread among cell phones, smart phones, handheld computers and pagers. CTI evolves beyond the confines of a stationary environment into responding to dynamic environments that merging mobile customers now create.

We are currently in a stage where CTI application such as screen pops and conditional call routing are being implemented in a majority of companies. To create greater capital investment efficiencies, economics will drive the convergence of applications riding on high-speed backbones and local area networks.

CT's successes will be in integrated applications, not in the development of features. Microsoft's greatest accomplishment wasn't in the development of all of those annoying paperclip features, it was integration of the various applications: Word, PowerPoint, Excel and Outlook. CT's challenges today are the cost of implementation, a lack of local expertise and steep learning curve for internal resources. For the next 36 months these application integration demand trends will be the principle drivers of the emergence of the vendor-neutral third party CT systems integrator.

This emerging market segment will be based on developing skill sets and application experiences around integrating IP functionality to legacy equipment. I characterize this as the "starfishing" market segment; technology and application experience with legs that extended into both emerging (IP) and legacy (circuit) technologies. Economy drives this as the costs of CT are still prohibitive, however these costs will drop as end-users utilize more of their data infrastructure to support their CT infrastructure.

Further supporting this emerging market expertise is that fact that CTI software and hardware will continue to see its highest growth in non-formal call centers. We will also see continued growth for at least 36 months in small to medium-sized businesses, although convergence is still too pricey for small business today –not as a consequence of hardware costs, but implementation costs.

In order to bring CTI into the mainstream we have to serve smaller offices, less than 100 employees, because they represent 90 percent of the growth opportunity. Specific market demand for the next 18 months will be for more intelligence in the applications that route engagements and generate responses to customers.

Specific high opportunity CTI application segments will be:

Email – Email growth, as a reliable transaction medium, will be governed by its evolution. However, evolutionarily it has a long way to go as email today still has far different expectations than phone calls. Does your company's internet address create the same expectation as your company's 1-800 number?

Chat - The fax machine, the telephone and e-mail are perfect examples of technologies that communicate with each other via standard protocols, regardless of manufacturer or origin. In this class of common communications mediums should be, and will be soon, instant messaging. Electronic chat (let's call it "e-chat"), or instant messaging, will emerge rapidly to be a powerful form of online customer communication, arriving well ahead of even IP based telephony.

Internet – Customers often know more about your company's products, service, offerings, and their account, than the people they talk to. Growth here will be in the integration of contact information and consequences with the contact management systems at employee desktops.

Dialing systems – When the technology sheds its "telemarketing interruptus" image and is applied to sustaining proactive two-way dialogues with customers. There is an integration opportunity with email when enterprises realize that email does not have to be responded to with email or phone calls responded to with phone calls. This is integrated media blending.

Workflow – Workflow is the manifestation of managing the concept of a customer's "demand unit." Ideally, workflow is the single application that follows this "demand unit" through the enterprise until it achieves a closure state. This includes tightly integrated queues incorporating work blending and load balancing of multiple media types. Also demands integration with marketing systems with personalized routing and work-object handling.

Virtual centers – Virtual centers consist of flexible work locations and remote workers.

Reporting – Reporting fully integrates reporting blending all queues and media types. Reporting follows the demand unit, not the queues or transactional efficiencies. Metrics around customer lifetime value, peripheral influence and loyalty emerge.

IVR – Interactive Voice Response evolves into Voice Response Systems that evolves into Speech Recognition that evolves into Near Simultaneous Language Translation. As companies globalize their businesses, language translation becomes a key issue. We can already do email language translation, so verbal language translation isn't conceivably too difficult. This is a function of processor horsepower more than anything.

Employee Desktop – This includes the capability to access internal and external data rapidly regardless of desktop location, to have customer parity (see what they see), and ability to execute transactions.

Call and Transaction Monitoring – As the conversations with customers contain the currency of the information age, so these dialogues will contain powerful insights about effective articulations from the agents and workers. Not only does enabling the customer feedback loop become important, the agent feedback loop becomes critical as well. This becomes particularly acute as the human resource becomes a more expensive and key competitive differentiator.

Telecom and data networks can no longer remain independent and have a significant impact or influence on customer focused applications and technologies today. From a technology evolution perspective, we are now most certainly moving into an implementation experience stage. With rare exceptions, economics will continue to drive not only the integration of new applications with legacy platforms but also the pace at which this technology is accepted by the consumer. CTIs future is one of sublimation into a much larger picture. We often discuss this under the guise of convergence.

Chapter Seven
Forward Thinkings

The following is a compilation of the Forward Thinking column written for 12 months from January, 2000 to December 2000 for Customer Interface Magazine and is reprinted with permission by Advanstar.

Forward Thinking
January 2000

About futurists, my two favorite quotes are, "Forecasting is a very difficult thing to do — especially about the future, " and the other sage Freeman Dyson said, "When it comes to useful futurists, it is better to be wrong than to be vague." So, here I am being asked to be a futurist, which can be a very slippery thing because the permanence of putting any prediction in writing eludes the safety most futurists find in the short memories of the masses. What I will try to do in this space is to make certain that you, the readers, don't make decisions in denial; denials about trends, shifts, and the application of technologies that are often seemingly unrelated, but influential in remarkable ways.

Throwing and reading the bones (how did you think futurists do it?) tells me that the meta-trend for the year 2000 will be around information; it's capture, storage and manipulation. Information is becoming the real currency of the digital age. One source of pure raw information, currency, is when companies talk to their customers and talking happens in call centers. That true power will come from the information that technology can generate and this makes call centers revenue engines. In fact it is the whole shift from product thinking to information thinking that obsoleting the contrast between call centers being a profit center or a cost center. The endemic pathology of call centers today is one of too much information and not enough sense. However, it is those customer conversations where the new currency—the big bills—of the information age is being minted. Bank on it.

Assuming that we all survive unscathed from the evolutionarily digital Darwinism of the Y2K bug (where all the right clocks will have gotten cleaned anyway), pay attention to the touch-points that your customers and employees use. Be aware that wireless technology is growing as fast, if not faster, than the internet. Keep your eye, perhaps better said your ears, on the intelligent edge of peripheral devices, as this is where customer evolution is really happening. The year 2000 is likely to prove out to be, not the year of the internet, but the year of the pervasive wireless device. And when all of your customers are paying by the minute to talk to you, you had better learn to be at least as lean and efficient as your competitors.

And long after satellites, fiber wireless, and the internet have proven to be more than just a prediction, enterprises will need to figure out a way to talk to those customers too. So, if you think that speech recognition is a novelty now, wait until you hear near-simultaneous natural language translation. I've been to the labs and heard the results and we are not too far away. Besides we can already do language translation of email, language is not that big of a leap ahead.

And these customers we will increasingly be communicating with are the emerging demand generation and they have only adopted the internet, they have internalized it. In a service culture driven by the mantra, "webify or die" this is a net-set culture of customers that speeds between web sites with the ease and alacrity of gazelles. The next new generation of customers has a whole new set of behaviors. This is the internet-powered generation devoid of segmentation by age; they have been raised on email and they don't need friendly face-to-face service. They want comprehensive accurate information, plenty of choices, competitive prices, and no-strings. Most important is that they consider their personal data to be valuable and they expect you to as well. Time is fast becoming their most precious commodity and substituting activity for achievement has become their biggest fear. To them, it is no longer about how fast you answer the phone but how well you know them.

For some time to come the internet will continue to create an explosion of telephone calls only to compound the pounding from demanding customers. What the internet has really done for customer service is to enable the customer to be increasingly more knowledgeable about your company's products and services than the very agents with whom they talk.

So what about these agents, the human-ware in the battery farms of the information age? Gold-collar workers or white collar slaves? Seventy to ninety percent of what happens in customer engagements is driven by human nature and has absolutely nothing to do with technology. There is a huge challenge ahead if we expect intelligence applied to those customer dialogues from a generation of net-workers grown up influenced by infotainment, docu-dramas and pop curricula manifesting itself in functional semi-literacy.

Certainly, it is with this next generation of human-ware where we will see the most radical of changes taking place. Successful service companies will be call centers built on hiring for intelligence because customers will expect, rather demand, for them to do much more than just be authorized to apologize. A consequence will be that, to play harder, you will have to pay more. It is no coincidence that "miser" is the root word of "miserable" and most of the misery of call centers, such as churn, can be all but slowed to a dribble when companies begin to pay more and hire for intelligence—it's more productive in the long run. Another myopic tendency of call centers is to deny that what the gold collar workers want is not a pension, but an education. Don't promise them a career; guarantee them employability.

Fortunately, when it comes to enterprises, customers, loyalty and profits, we can be fairly certain that the future is fairly binary; it's either evolution or extinction. Survival—digital even—requires acknowledging that not everything that has worked in the past will work in the future. The web-year pace of the future will be slowed by cultures weighted down by their own historical inertia. In a myopic and cynical sense, there is a whole lot of evolutionary irony wrapped up in things such as Erlangs and telephones. So be careful that the technology you invest in today does not contradict the very efficiencies you think that you will achieve tomorrow because in the customer service chain, it is no longer be about how fast you can react, it is about how far out you can think.

Those unfortunates that fail to survive, companies and people, will be those that could not, or would not, take the bull by the horns and grasp the fact that the new rules are there are no rules. For survival call centers will require the very same corporate entrepreneurial fervor as any other successful division.

Success in our call center industry will come when we realize that we are no longer in the business of implementing technology and managing people, we are in the business of implementing change. It is no longer about cost justification and best business practices; it is about change justification and smart business practices.

Evolution has a particularly humorous irony to it and the bones clearly warn us to beware of self-perpetuating buzz word traps and to clearly understand that aggregating eyeballs and increasing stickiness are often just slogans masquerading as strategy. Even the sales of drill bits are continuing to grow as fast as many technologies. But of the tens of millions of drill bits sold every year—like technology—what people really still want are just the holes. The future is in the holes.

Forward Thinking
February 2000

If you know your history the future will not trouble you. - African Proverb

For the past eight years Stanley Brown, a Partner with PriceWaterhouseCoopers, has been doing an on-going study called the *Ideas Survey* that defines the evolutionary stages of customer care. In this fascinating study, PriceWaterhouseCoopers regularly surveys some 15,000 businesses and has come to the conclusion that there are three identifiable stages of customer care evolution.

In the first stage, which PWCoopers called the "Customer Acquisition" stage, sixteen percent of the companies surveyed were found to fall into this Stage One category. Like a stereotypical car dealership, I would suggest that these 16 percent of companies exhibit institutional behaviors such as that of hunters. They are focused on slaying customers and eating them with little or no after thought about ever servicing them again.

The second stage of Customer Care was "Customer Relationship Management." A whopping 76 percent of the companies fell into this category. I characterize this stage as ranchers. Ranchers do a little better job than the hunters, they invest and take time to fatten you up first and then they eat you. In this stage of company, the idea of lifetime customer relationship value is valid all the way up until the customer is eaten, but for the most part, not much further than that.

The Third Stage is defined as "Strategic Customer Care." A particularly impressionable 8 percent of companies made the cut. I consider this stage farmers. These farmers have a particularly acute sense of the idea of sustained yield management. These companies are in the thirty percent of companies that are actually using computer telephone integration to exploit the use of customer data. Farmers are driven to retain customers season after season. In these companies there is a sophisticated and high degree of appreciation for the information potential of call centers. Here, call centers are a proof point of the evolution of customer care.

I'd be interested to know how many of you believe that you are in that eight percent farmer stage? Stan Brown thinks as many as one-third of you (I think it is higher) actually think you are in the Stage Three (Farmer). Bottom line, a good number of call center people think that they doing a better job of incorporating life-time value strategies into the day-to-day operations of call centers, than they really are.

Now what about the future? I have expanded Stanley's Customer Care Stages to five.

The Fourth Stage I would consider to be Vegetarians. These are enterprises marked by information consistency and media parity, meaning that no matter in which media a customer engages, the information is consistent. During a several minute exercise not to long ago, I called my bank and discovered that an account balance the IVR gave me was different than the balance the agent gave me and both were different from my balance on-line. I would like to know if you consider yourself to be a Stage Four company, I suspect that there are only rare handfuls.

These stage four companies will have an articulate grasp of the value of the information that the call center generates. And, unlike old adversarial mass media, instead of realizing revenues in selling the information they collect, these Vegetarians will push the information from every customer dialogue and engagement back into the enterprise in a continuous feedback stream. These companies won't eat customers; they eat the information customers generate. These are enterprises where the information about a transaction becomes more valuable than the transaction itself.

The Fifth Customer Care Stage is the Breath-atarians. Give this stage thirty or more years to develop and it is entirely plausible that digital agents will become entirely indistinguishable from live ones. The idea of customer lifetime value becomes a worn concept replaced by the idea of generational value. My grandfather, my father, my son, and myself are all customers of the same insurance company (USAA). I am so operationally entangled with them that it would indeed take generations and a lot of bad service to unravel the relationship. In Japan, there are mortgage companies that are offering 100-year mortgages. Now that is generational entanglement.

A conclusive characteristic of all of these evolving enterprises is their shift from accomplishing extraordinary transactional efficiencies to fulfilling deep customer relational intimacies. The fact is that today the concept of CRM very much contradicts the very efficiencies that most call centers strive to achieve. The PriceWaterhouseCoopers Ideas Survey reflects a natural evolutionary adaptation from technology and product thinking to information and relationship thinking. The consequences of this evolution are brutally real.

Evolution requires change and, with call centers, that can be hard to do because there is so much of it to change. This evolution starts with the intellectual integrity to admit that our enterprises may not be quite as customer conscious as we think we are.

Forward Thinking
March 2000

When we have evolved well past CRM, one-to-one marketing, mass customization and personalization, and these constructs have become internalized into every customer engagement, what will we evolve to next? I have a pretty good idea and it includes the notion that the enterprise's dependence on the call center and its agents will become greater, much greater, not less.

A significant flaw in the idea of one-to-one customer relationship management is that it only takes into account the value of a customer in dollars. We seek the Pareto customer, that 20% that accounts for 80% of our revenues. The failure is that there is not a mathematical algorithm in the world or a room full of MBA's with calculators that can account for the fact that, while I may be a low dollar value customer, I might just be a high-influence customer (or conversely, a high-value, but highly obnoxious customer).

The next evolutionary step in CRM will be the identification of very fine opportunity segments where customers are not segmented based on their fiscal value, which is a fairly sophisticated concept when you begin to calculate a customers lifetime value, or even generational value (there are companies in Japan offering 100 year mortgages), but on other more important, relative values. The valuation of customers will evolve to become quite subjective and the only time that this can happen is at the time of the dialogue between the agent and the customer.

I have a dear friend that owns a first class moving company. He flies less than twenty thousand miles a year on Continental Airlines, but every time he flies he pays for and takes a crew with him. So, while he may not travel enough miles to obtain the vaulted Gold Elite status, he buys enough tickets that Continental gave him Gold status anyway. This makes sense, but it torque's me because last year I flew 40,000 miles, all of them exclusively on Continental Airlines and I didn't get gifted Gold status.

You see, what Continental Airlines has the opportunity to do is recognize that, although I am not a high dollar value customer measured in miles, I am a high-influence customer. Not only do I enjoy the pulpit of this column, but I also traveled those miles to speak for maybe 10,000 people about customer service and call centers. If you have heard me speak, you have heard my Continental Airlines story.

How do you identify these segments? Just ask me.

As the power of technology evolves to enable every company to keep track of each and every dialogue we have with its customers, it will be the information gleaned from those conversations that will truly drive the building of loyal, long-term, and profitable relationships. You cannot script the intimate conversations that will be required to glean the types of powerful insights about how customers needs and preferences are evolving over time. In fact, the very core tenet of CRM actually contradicts the efficiencies we strive to achieve in call centers today.

Determining the value of a customer's influence is a subjective decision that only can be made at the time of the dialogue with an agent. Every time I make a reservation with Continental I mention that I know just a little bit about call centers and that I travel frequently to give presentations about call centers and customer service. You would think that they would take note.

Theoretically, Continental Airlines (your company) has the ability to identify that population of customers that has a disproportionate influence unrelated to their fiscal value. Continental Airlines should make that population all Gold Elite status; Platinum status, if they want to make sure that my five year old kid becomes a loyal customer in fifteen years.

The relative importance of agents in customer engagements will grow, not diminish, with the personalization of technology. The technology of call centers can help us capture and guide those dialogues, but only agents can create them. And if you think that you are going to have informational and intimate dialogues with agents paid $8.00 per hour, you will miss the evolutionary mark by a mile.

One-to-one marketing applied to the call center, although steeply mired in monetary perspective today, will evolve into relying on the intelligent, conversational and very subjective decision making skills of an entire new class of call center agent.

Did you hear me Continental?

Forward Thinking
May 2000

"Labor became a factor of production, then a cog in industrial machinery and now a willing slave in the electronic sweatshop."

-Let M Eknow

A dangerous trend is that customer service chain executives increasingly are buying into the myth that information technology can store human intelligence or distribute human experience. We are consistently missing the fact that while technology gets 90 percent of the attention, it is still humans that do 85 percent of the work. We have certainly evolved to the point where we can do the machine-to-machine interface really well and we even do a good job sometimes at the machine to human piece. However, it is with the human-to-human interface that we will see the most radical, and occasionally catastrophic, changes will take place in the next few short years. Unionization, gold collar workers paid $90 per hour, the complexity of their demands, and hiring for intelligent conversation are a couple of trends to watch.

Unionization

In a very Orwellian sense, we are fast creating a clear distinction between the gold collar worker and the white collar slave. When the Communication Workers of America turn their attention to call center agents, it will be because there is no longer the need to look after the interests of people who string wire from pole to pole.

Expense

If you think that technology is expensive today, wait until you find out what you will have to pay for the people that use it tomorrow. The people you expect to talk to customers are talking to customers who often know more about your company than the very agents they talk to. Calls are getting harder, not easier and faster. The internet in fact is creating an explosion, not lessening, of calls. It is no coincidence that the word miser is the root word of miserable and enterprises must clearly understand that one sure formula for failure is paying $6.00 an hour for conversations and expecting $25 an hour intelligence. Hire for intelligence because they are handling customer knowledge, the currency of the information age.

Hire Conversationalists

It is within conversations with customers where the real data diamonds lie. Evolved companies will obtain deep insights from conversations with customers. What the internet really enables today is customer conversations about the promises companies are making, or breaking. We rarely take the time to listen because the idea of "customer relationship management" (xRM) fundamentally contradicts the very efficiencies that call centers strive to achieve. You want agents to talk to customers longer. You cannot script the intimacies that will drive these conversations because scripting dumbs down conversations. You cannot have an intelligent conversation between an agent and the customer when an agent asks questions such as, "Was that 'n' as in knife?" Or better, if that was "Q as in cucumber?" Hire intelligent conversationalists, because the very best call centers in the world just might be a roomful of web-literate grandmothers who love to chat. ("Sweetie, just reboot your PC and I always add _ teaspoon of vanilla more than what the recipe calls for.")

Demands

No one grows up wanting to be a call center agent. Unionized or not, the agent of the future will be known as the "demand generation" and they will not see themselves as interfaces; they're decision makers. They want to work in small groups and be a part of every decision. Direct orders set them on edge and you will not earn their respect by not doing what they do. You must explain why it is you want them to do something, or even better, show them.

Kathleen Peterson, consultant from Bedford, NH, makes the observations in a recent white paper that agents today, "Don't want a pension, they want an education. They don't want a 401k, they want employability." She astutely suggests that we should teach them something nonself-serving like algebra or Shakespeare because there is a good chance some of your agents have kids needing help with their homework.

"When the world turns a little," as one of my favorite consultants, Toni Bayche says, "human resources will become so expensive and scarce, that technology will adapt with neural networks, adaptive logic, and fuzzy algorithms." Don Greco with Siemens ICN thinks that call center based commerce will become about markets where there are no agents, no supervisors, or no call centers—no centers of anything—just professionals focused and informed through powerful networked technology and applications.

Not only is this shift imminent, but it will most certainly and profoundly overturn every existing customer relationship. The overall culture of the call center will then change dramatically, if not catastrophically, forcing focused attention on new approaches to hiring, training, managing, and keeping the gold collar worker.

Forward Thinking
June 2000

Part of being a futurist, at least one that can squeak out a living at it, isn't figuring out about what comes next, it's about figuring our how fast what comes next gets here. It is easy to say that humans will walk on Mars; the difficulty is in predicting exactly when that walk will happen.

One of the influences on how fast these things get here is an understanding of how much drag there is on the pace change. Change, particularly in our business, is not aerodynamic and the future does not look like anything like a smooth and symmetrical bell curve.

Legacy hesitation has an incredibly underestimated influence on the pace of adoption of customer facing technology. The adoption rate of devices and interfaces that customers will use for service is no different than the adoption of the technologies of music, gaming and television. If you are not paying attention to the devices your kids are using, you may be clueless about what your customers may be using. The definition and expectations of customer service become very different when Nintendo becomes a bank, which they are actually considering.

In the pace of web-years, there are only a handful of "laws" that have emerged with any veracity. One is Moore's Law (the doubling of processing power every 18 months) and the second is Metcalfs Law (the quadratic growth in value of the internet). And while these two are influential peripherally to customer service, it is the other Moore's Law that carries all of the real weight.

Geoffrey Moore wrote a book in 1991 called *Crossing the Chasm.* In it he basically said that technology adoption isn't a neat and tidy bell curve. No, to him technology adoption is snail shaped. What I want to suggest is that not only is the adoption of technology snail shaped, it undulates randomly and the curves themselves actually flatten out with time. I believe that this flattening out will continue to happen for some time to come.

Martha Rogers (of 1:1 authorship) says that television penetration in ghettos is higher than the telephone penetration. If your customers live in ghettos, then you need to learn to talk to them through their televisions. It wasn't but a few short years ago that some nine percent of the US was still using rotary telephone circuits. If those rotary telephone users are your customers, IVR and web pages are useless, but speech recognition may work astonishingly well.

Forrester Research suggests that most pure online retailing ventures will crash and burn by next year because of competition and a lack of sufficient funding. Heated and crushing competition from Walmart, Sears, and Home Depot will prove that the bricks will drive the clicks, not the other way around.

The Gartner Group estimates that (.8 probability) 35 percent of all commerce by 2003 will be electronic. That's amazing growth, and I agree with this prediction. But, let's not ignore the fact that this still leaves 65 percent something else and this something else is the telephone, more specifically voice and conversation. The perceived pace of change in how customers want to talk to you – and they do indeed want to talk to you, is happening well in front of the actual pace of change.

The point I want to leave you with is this, when you intersect all of these trends you discover that the hype far exceeds the reality.

In the last two thousand people I have talked to I have asked them if they are using—not experimenting with, it's not a novelty—but are actually using IP telephones. Remarkably, only a handful ever raised their hands. The media-zation of call center technology–which is neither good nor bad—is at work here. And while the internet gets all of the attention (press), call centers are still doing all of the work.

There are many deep reasons for this effect. One is that it takes an absolute misunderstanding of human nature to believe that people would ever prefer automated transactions over live human ones. Humans do seek efficiency, but you and I are increasingly aware of who is trivializing our customer relationships and who is not. Conversations about this trivialization are exactly what the internet now enables.

As the markets are currently beginning to prove, bricks will drive the clicks. It still takes quite a few bricks; call centers specifically, to provide the excellent customer service that your competitors are providing.

Forward Thinking
July 2000
The Decentralization of Call Centers
I wouldn't be much of a useful futurist if all I ever did was parrot back what most other futurists say. They more often than not just tell you that you have to think outside of the box, but give you little practical or pragmatic advice on just exactly how to do that. Indeed, I think that the most useful futurist is one who not only talks about what's next, but more importantly, tells you precisely how fast what's next is going to get here.

The inevitability of the virtual call center, or the cyber call center is fairly certain. We can all easily envision a time when the agents of the company become so remote they do indeed become truly virtual. What is not so certain is whether this will happen by 2010 or by 2050. I do predict (1.0 probability) that there will be a whole dictionary of buzzwords and acronyms around the technology of the distributed call center. A definition itself that has already been bogged down by it's own vernacular morass with the likes of IVR, CTI, ACD, PBX, and currently xRM.

Today, it is on the peripheral of call centers, within the applications of gaming, entertainment and collaboration that we can see the fundamental experience customers will have in the near future.

Collaboration applications play a big part in the complex formula of customer service because eventually the technologies that we use to talk to our agents and employees become the same applications that we use to talk to our customers.

Look at the gaming industry, specifically the games our children play, to understand what happens when customers substitute "avatars" and "characters" for "real" humans. What happens when the applications of technology in call centers gets to the point where a customer cannot tell the difference between live and Memorex.

Entertainment will teach us to enthrall customer eyeballs with intoxicating content (remember Victoria's Secret on-line?).

The eventual "distributed call center" will be that, but it will be neither virtual, nor remote. What we will see more likely is a hybrid, a retail type location and environment. Shopping centers, strip commercial developments, and highway corridors will be the locations of these nodes (for lack of a better description) of skilled and technically literate call center agents. The large enterprise will remain but in the form of many more locations draped over the backbone of glass and supporting even smaller and smaller groups of agents.

We will also find that the further out you go geographically from technology concentrations (cities basically), the greater the expense, not just of the technology, but of the human ware as well. The further the enterprises intellectual capital from centralized technology, the greater the necessary bandwidth, and of course, the greater the expense.

We know that one of the challenges with managing large centralized call centers today is with the requirement for a large labor pool. Unfortunately, with the larger labor pool comes a less skilled population to select from. The smart people you want working for you and talking to your customers don't want to live in big cities.

What will drive the decline of the large centralized call center is the realization that we are in many cases, in various degrees of just throwing sophisticated technology at ignorant people. When we employ technology that increases frustration instead of creating efficiencies, we have a Siebelism (which is completely different from Netwonization). In a practical sense you can't exploit the advantages of xRM using $9.00 an hour agents.

It's the human-to-human piece of the equation that will matter the most because while we spend 90 percent of our time talking about the technology, 90 percent of the formula has to do with the people, the human ware. Better paid agents are smarter agents who accomplish more and like it. Think of stockbrokers, they are in a sense call center agents with extra-ordinary salaries. This futurist expects a time when cradle to grave customer service becomes so important in culture that we actually pay prized call center agents like sports stars.

The fact is that the largest influence on the advent of the truly distributed call center will have little to do with technology and mostly to do with people, because distributed call centers perfectly combat agent poaching, agent churn and create employee loyalty by lessening commutes (greening their jobs).

Call centers are the proof point for the pragmatic application of technology. As chips and networks get bigger and faster, the engagements we have with customers get bigger (important) and more critical. Loyalty is affected by the consistency of the customer's experience with you. How come FedEx can know the status of a package by the hour but my bank actually thinks that I believe that it still takes five days to collect on out-of-state checks? Doesn't my bank realize that they now compete with FedEx?

As technology gets better at networking, mostly a function of bandwidth, it will also become more complex. Understanding the intersection between technical complexity, the need for distributed intelligence, the availability of an digitally intelligent labor pool, and the peculiars of your particular industry and this should give you solid triangulation in on the true pace of the decentralization evolution.

Forward Thinking
August 2000

Several months ago my lovely wife and CEO Cheryl was talking to a company that we do business with through their 800 number. Near the beginning of the conversation the agent asked her if she was an AOL subscriber (she wasn't). Curious about this query I discovered that, had she been an AOL subscriber, they would have next asked her to log on and continue the conversation through a "chat session" or "instant messaging." Why? Because unlike the more expensive 800 number phone call at sixteen cents per minute, the chat session was relatively free.

The fax machine, the telephone and e-mail are perfect examples of technologies that communicate with each other via standard protocols, regardless of manufacturer or origin. In this class of common communications mediums should be, and will be soon, instant messaging. The popularity and speedy uptake of instant messaging as a communications medium with your customers will blindside most of us. As a futurist I am expecting that electronic chat (let's call it "e-chat"), or instant messaging, will emerge rapidly to be a powerful form of online customer communication, arriving well ahead of even IP based telephony.

Instant messaging is a classic case of "we have the technology, it's something else that prevents its adoption." It should be no surprise that it is an issue of standards clearly clouding chat's evolutionary waters. AOL has some 90 million users signed up on "buddy lists." This allows users to send and receive messages between members faster than email. AOL has blocked its members from receiving messages from applications that are not partnered with AOL. Many feel that when AOL gets unblocked (including anti-trust interests in the Federal Government - hey, if they can take down Microsoft, why not TW/AOL?), the hope is that all instant message applications will connect to all others in no different of commonness as email, fax and telephones.

There will be three versions of this chat stuff relevant to our business. The first is when the customer initiates chat; i.e. "I'm looking at your web page, do you have the widgets in blue?" Another variation would be the instant windows that "pop" chat messages to customers as they navigate through your website. The third, and most valuable will be the instant feedback chat.

In this digital age information is currency. Don't you think that somebody in your company wants to know if product descriptions are through and complete, if navigating the site is simple and whether or not the site downloads quickly? Shouldn't the call center be collecting information on the quality of the company web site instead of the web site collecting information on the quality of the call center?

Chat from a web site will emerge to be considered the internet's most critical service. In the evolution of call centers, agents must learn the skill sets required to communicate this way, like good spelling. This is critical because unlike email chat isn't something that you spell check. You cannot script chat sessions, they are spontaneous and free flowing and in the context of a call center they will require agents who are thoroughly knowledgeable about your products and services.

Instant messaging is currently in the purgatory between good news and bad news. The bad news is that one of the most powerful forms of internet based customer communications is already here, but standards and connectivity squabbles (mostly between AOL and everybody else), not technology, is preventing it from being deployed.

The good news is that you have a short period of time to get ready for this next new customer communications channel demand. Unfortunately, many of us will miss this opportunity because while the press, magazines, and trade shows are about everything else glamorous, instant messaging, like telephones, IVR, and voice mail will still be doing all of the work.

Forward Thinking
September 2000

There was a recent column in a next-generation networks magazine written by some sage pundit discussing the ultimate dissolution of every technology that ever lived. "Decomposition" was exactly how he described it. I don't think that evolution happens in such a macabre way.

I find the description of star fishing more appropriate. Star fishing is the extension into untenable directions always with one or more legs firmly attached in the direction of the past. Some species of starfish and companies survive quite well with this strategy. The most successful CRM companies are the ones that have been providing technology the longest—Siemens, Nortel, and Lucent, for example. There are a lot of amazing technologies and companies out there today, but it is the ones with the depth off of the bench that have the clear competitive advantage because they are the ones that know how to reinvent themselves, even after losing a leg or two.

The traditional idea of a call center involves a very old technology called an ACD (automatic call distributor). ACD's are very much a "brick" type technology as in the "bricks and mortar". Call centers are bricks because they remain hugely capital intensive, they must interface with every conceivable communications device a customer could use (from rotary to laptop) and they are sources of huge complexity and bureaucracy, yet they are still considered a fundamental building block of any enterprise's customer service strategy.

Today's ACD isn't anywhere near as dumb as a brick. This "ACD" is where your company gathers a fundamental critical form of information about where and how your company as a whole should be evolving. If you are truly listening to your customers, then you know exactly what to do next. But, don't fail to understand that star fishing the customer service technology evolution has little to do with technology or infrastructure; it's now much deeper than that. It's about your company's culture—its depth off of the bench.

Getty Images is a Seattle based company demonstrably star fishing itself into the future. Its customers are advertising firms, agencies, newspapers, magazines, and other visual artists. They are a business firmly rooted in an old technology—the atoms of film and photographs—media that have no place in the superfluidity of business in the digital age.

Getty is hustling, mostly by acquisition, to replace the atoms of paper catalogs and celluloid based film into the bits and bytes of web sites. In the old days, the process of copying film costs $238 per image, today digitizing a photo costs $45, with nothing to ever duplicate again, except hard drives. Customers do key word searches of the web-based catalog and view uncorrected and rough images. A credit card is all it takes to purchase the images you want. You begin to download the image immediately (warning: don't try this at 24 kps!). What took a month, now takes minutes—nothing but net. But it wasn't always such a slam dunk.

The biggest challenge for Getty, and it may still be, is that there was a culturally embedded form of legacy hesitation that genuinely feared that the reverence for photography would be corrupted and lost forever. This ultimately has proven to be unfounded.

The point is, not a single recent article or description of Getty neglects to mention the critical importance of Getty's call center full of "research specialists." These agents help customers find images from Getty's catalogue of some 70 million images – a catalogue that is growing at some 750 images every 12 hours. Getty's goal is to answer 93% of its 6,000 inbound calls per week in less than one minute. This almost makes me want to be a customer. Getty's success isn't in just making it into the 21st century alive and kicking, it's that they have done it using call centers, star fishing.

Getty is using a remarkably old technology, ACDs, to provide brand spanking new digital quality service. Getty gets it.

In our business, xRM is really more about a culture change, not a technology change. It's pessimistic to think that things just decompose. No, they just get sucked up in the tidal backwash of the digital age and get spit back out all shiny and buffed. Somewhere in your enterprise someone is driving to create a culture that is digital, creative, spontaneous and consistent. Call centers will always be responsible for the consistent part. Customer service chain executive's success will come from creating and perpetuating this culture of consistency.

Star fishing is how successful people and enterprises will survive the constant renewal of rules and order—one leg at a time.

Forward Thinking
October 2000

Want to know who is the best queue manager in the world? I was convinced that it was Disney World for many years, now I am convinced that it's McDonalds, Burger King and Wendy's.

It is ironically stupefying to discover that call centers are remarkably like McDonald's. That can be both good and bad. The truth is that the fast food industry has a lot to teach customer service chain executives because most fast food restaurants make burgers better and faster than most companies take orders and give answers.

McDonald's, the largest restaurant chain in the world has some 1.5 million agents. The french fry has continued to be for many years the most respected item on the McDonald's menu. Recently McDonald's came up with a new cooking system that will make a batch of fries in 65 seconds compared to the old way that took 210 seconds. This means a lot when saving time is important. Every six seconds saved at a McDonald's drive-through means a sales increase of 1 percent. Increasing drive through efficiency by ten percent will increase sales on average by $54,000 per year per store. In some places toll tags can be used to pay for items, shaving another 15 seconds off of drive through time and increasing sales by another two percent!

Burger King now wants to be able to "beat the car to the window with the food." Someday maybe call centers will try as hard.

Customer experiences with superb queue speeds are all around us. In a society where we are queued up everywhere we go, banks, grocery stores, and gas stations, speed has become a noticeably competitive influence.

Speed can create an emotional attachment to a company. Wendy's knows that when customer service times are below 130 seconds, customers especially notice that service is fast. But when Wendy's consistently gets below 100 seconds per order, they discovered that they got an emotional attachment from their customers. This emotional attachment evolves to become an expectation of speedy service that involves your company's brand. See the connection here? Regular customers at one restaurant's drive-through with six cars in line will know that they are likely to move faster in that line than a three-car line at the competitor across the street.

There is a down side to the metrics of fast food and call center efficiencies. Speed only counts if you get it right. Accuracy is usually the biggest price to pay for accomplishing speed. Because, while Wendy's does it fast, they don't get it right, at least enough to be ranked 11th in order accuracy. We all know, like Wendy's does, that quality *is* your speed limit.

Don't make the mistake of doing it fast, but getting it wrong, which is the same as substituting activity for achievement. Think like a customer and remember that sinking feeling when we discovered that the food order is messed up and you got somebody else's greasy taco instead of the veggie pita.

Real world customers aren't dumb. There are enough companies out there that do such a bad job with technology that the media propaganda about great service does not match our experiences. We know that at hotels and supermarkets we still wait in line the same time as we used to wait.

When I was a teenager I took a nasty spill on my skateboard going 80 mph, (ok maybe forty). I experienced the ugly phenomena of speed wobble until I finally let go and slid the last thirty feet on my hands and knees. Speed is good until you get speed wobble. Tampering with customers and the way you talk to them can backfire in extraordinarily unexpected ways. For the same reason we don't experiment with our customers, McDonald's hesitates to take chances with their french fries.

On a global scale, the future fear that I have is that call centers will grow in repute as factories of white-collar slaves—cubical-cized, Nike-like factory workers of the information age. Life in call centers is like life in fast food, it is short lived. Living by a clock and churning out information like burgers and where blowing time budgets by 25 seconds creates unproductive stress, explains a 200 percent per year churn.

Unfortunately, most speed records are almost always broken by people with no place in particular to go. My kendo sensei says that slower is harder. So true. Evolution in call centers comes when it is realized that if it is speed you want, then it is viscosity you'll need.

Forward Thinking
November 2000

Forewarned is forearmed.

Markets crave philosophies – it's the supraliminal justification for their purpose. Profitable business plans always need philosophical bow waves to propel, and often compel, them forward. It is how investments are justified in the absence of hard cash returns.

There has never been a better time to be a customer or a more painful time to be a company. Customers are in control.

First of all, let's agree that this isn't an internet charged economy, this is a customer charged economy. Customers are in control. Technology, particularly the internet, does that to people. They have access to and can retrieve more information from the internet than ever before.

This is what the internet does to customers–it knowledgifies them. Customers now know more about your company, its products, and services, than the company representatives they talk to. This knowledge-fied customer is an emerging demographic, devoid of segmentation by age, that knows exactly what they want and how they want to get it – and they got money.

These are customers now demanding control of their relationships with you, not the other way around. The things that customers want today are not the things that customers wanted yesterday. This is the Demand Generation and these are your customers.

Tomorrow, customer managed relationships will be dynamically formed on the fly. Technology, especially the internet, not only creates discriminating companies, it creates discriminating customers. Increasingly, the customer, not the company, will determine loyalty. Customers are in control.

Most companies will be knocked over sober, if they manage to get up at all, when they discover that the very idea of customer relationship management, CRM, insults their average customer. Customers don't want their relationships to be managed. To customers, customers manage relationships. Would you actually tell your customers that you believe that you actually manage them?

The whole idea of CRM, and its acronym too, is a nice piece of flagrant vendor speak designed to rise above market noise. Don't make the mistake of substituting slogans for strategy. In the case of CRM, itself fundamentally contradicts the efficiencies that we strive to achieve in call centers. Don't we really want agents to talk to customers for longer periods of time? I can't find a metric for that.

You used to create products and services for the customer, now they are telling us what they want us to do, exactly. But we are not listening to them. You have a terrific ROI because you hang up on customers faster and more efficiently than ever, but the return on your relationships at that moment, much less their lifetime, is pretty nil.

Today the metric is Return On Investment and the goal is customer satisfaction. Tomorrow, in the customer controlled economy, satisfaction will be a given. Customer satisfaction will merely be the ante required to play in the game. Payola is found in the loyalty.

What CRM should fear is that the idea of a return on customer relationships and customer managed demand be a tipping point as we relinquish the grip of traditional measures of customer satisfaction like Erlang. There is a supreme market advantage in thinking that future measures of success do not include Erlang.

It would be fairer to say that customers are in more control because obviously all of the power has not been turned over to the peasants. If customers can discriminate, than obviously so can companies. The internet now enables discriminating companies.

Today we have technology that keeps track of the information that comes out of customer conversations. When you begin to brand customers on a basis of one to one, you ultimately move to forms of pricing discrimination based on personality characteristics. Obnoxious whiners should be charged more than passively loyal customers. Demanding customers cost more.

When customers are in control they can demand all they want, and the successful companies will be the ones that give it to them.

Forward Thinking
December 2000

Geoffrey Moore wrote a seminal book in 1991 titled Crossing the Chasm. Ten years later he has been proven nearly dead-on when he wrote that technology adoption is not a smooth bell curve, it is, in fact, snail shaped with uneven and rough edges.

The "neck" of the snail, which some call the "trough of disillusionment" or the "early adopters", is where most technologies and it's applications fail. They fail because they do not calculate for the chiasmic difference between the growth of early adopters and the growth of the early majority. Burning resources too fast on the first group and underestimating what it takes to succeed in the latter, is what kills most companies and demonstrably impacts the adoption rate of many technologies and applications.

Let's look at e-tailing as an example. Forrester Research predicts that $3.2 trillion, 13% of U.S. retailing will be conducted on line by 2004. On-line retail sales will grow ten-fold in the next few years. While looking awestruck at the enormous growth of internet e-tailing ahead of us, we may be failing to calculate the depth of the chasm Geoffrey Moore's law predicts below.

Rarely will anyone disagree today that the current on-line backlash is driven by the absurd valuations of companies that can't get orders and service right and the equally absurd hype that they can. The consequence or cause of this simple fact is that very few of the dot coms are making any money at all.

Since these are not the market challenges of the market of bricks, the consequence is that established bricked-based companies are better positioned and more likely to succeed than new dot coms in the online world. Established companies have experience in the call center/warehousing/fulfillment/delivery/service chain.

While clicks may get all of the attention, bricks will do all of the work. Bricks will drive clicks.

Factoid: The top 706 publicly traded U.S. Internet firms employ 971,500 workers. WalMart alone has 1.1 million employees.

One of the tools of a futurist is that of triangulation. By studying the peripheral of any particular subject to understand new economy e-tailing, in this case traditional retailing, you can quickly build an accurate expectation of how fast what's next will get here. Considering that you likely thought you would ever see trigonometry again, here are six companies in various stages of e-chasms to triangulate with.

WalMart is experiencing double digit revenue growth and will open 300 more physical stores next year. Relative only to the effect of immensity, WalMart is expected to surpass General Motors in sales this year. Recently WalMart unexpectedly shut down their Internet on-line store for an unheard of "remodeling." Most other e-tailers constantly upgrade their old sites. WalMart's on-line development will profoundly alter the future of e-tailing because they get the most eyeballs off-line. WalMart will set the adoptive pace of technology, not Amazon.com.

General Motors is predicting that it will install 4 million in-car information devices by 2003. This is a lot of rolling bricks. This is the beginning of a whole new type of customer needing personalize service at 60 mph. Transactive speed and efficiency becomes critical for customer service demands from places we never had them from beforeæin this case from the inside of a car at high-speed. I expect that by 2005 nearly one-half of these outfitted cars will be wrecked by drivers checking email at the green light in front of you.

Sears has roots to 1880 and wouldn't exactly be considered a new-economy type of company. But Sears has been one of the most aggressive in bringing their online presence inline with their retail locations. Sears has discovered that one in ten appliance purchases are influenced by their on-line presence. Sears' best online sellers are big ticket items and it's number one browsed item and number one best seller is lawn mowers.

FedEx has always been in the business of bricks, most of them weighing less than two pounds. Today, two-thirds of its U.S. domestic transactions are handled on-line. Of the millions of two to ten pounds bricks FedEx handles daily, they have realized that the information about those bricks is often worth more than the bricks themselves.

Even pure on-line e-commerce companies such as Directbanking.com have moved from pure clicks to some bricks, having just built a three dimensional store front in the Financial District in downtown Boston. Amazon.com is more brick than most people realize with millions of square feet of warehouse space and 2,000 call center agents.

EasyJet is a low-cost airline that shuttles around 18 European cities. It sells an amazing 80 percent of its tickets directly on-line. EasyJet believes that they can be brick-less and next year is expecting to close down all of their call centers and handle all bookings on-line. I predict that EasyJet will have its call centers full of bricks open in less than 30 days.

Bricks will drive clicks as we now realize the extreme of expectations that technology and its applications are capable of creating. However, the dismantling and massive reorganizing of institutions, companies, and the enterprises of free markets, as we say in Texas, "Ain't gonna happen." The internet will not make all previous iterations of commerce irrelevant unless you are contrasting from fifteen or more years from now, just as TV didn't obsolete radio and MP3 won't obsolete CD's.

Momentum, of which mass is a component, influences what we do next. It will be brick oriented companies—the WalMarts, Home Depots, and Safeways of the world—that will propagate the successful elements of the new economy. In fact, the brick-based strategies of keeping costs down, using cutting edge technologies, and non-union work forces (hallmarks of WalMart), will carry even more strategic influence than ever.

Triangulation is one method futurists use to calculate the future. The flaw with this method is that a single critical function in the formula has been left out—your company. Ignore the hype and do the math, or in this case, the trigonometry.

Chapter Eight
Globility and Solutioning

The vendors of the technology and applications that interface with a businesses' most vital asset, its customers, are rapidly developing far-reaching, comprehensive (some would suggest dizzying), and complex ways to communicate with this most vital of all resources. The sweeping changes in the availability of channels, devices, and interfaces is happening at every level, in every enterprise, from the way your executives communicate with each other to the way your customers communicate with your call center.

As a proof point for this evolutionary change, we can observe traditional call center environments. Even the traditional call center environment is being radically changed, evolving from a one dimensional voice-intensive operation to an internet-based multimedia contact center that can accommodate not only telephone calls but internet-generated queries, e-mail, chat, and, emerging quickly, streaming media and video.

For the enterprise's customer relationships, the internet enables an unprecedented boon in service, timeliness, and personalization. The internet enables customers to serve themselves, set their own service schedules, and choose their preferred medium for communication and retrieving information—a practice that unquestionably deepens relationships.

Radical change isn't just external with internet enabled customers, but internal with development of business analytics and the leveraging of existing databases and customer backgrounds leading to the effective mining and deepening of existing relationships.

Call centers are an important proof point for the practical application of technology. Employing some 5 million workers and processing some 5 percent of the US Gross Domestic Product transactions per day, call centers are an incredibly vital part of the global economy. As a consequence of this vitalness, we can study call center environments to understand not only the impact and significance of emerging technologies, but the pace at which they are truly adopted.

Looking to the peripheral of call centers, we can identify three significant influences from a technology point of view. The first is globility, which is inclusive of the massive emergent market of wireless applications, particularly WAP (Wireless Application Protocol), and includes the enabling of a distributed workforce, tele-working in particular. The second significant influence is multi-channel customer relationship management; the third is application portability.

Mobility & Remote Technology Will Drive the Multi-Channel World

> **globility** \glō-'bil-et-ē\ *adj* : the ability of an enterprise to respond to the persistently changing demands of an increasing internationalized economy.

Globility is a large and encompassing concept and it is certainly much more than just the brief discussion of customer mobility found in this discourse. Mobility, depending on your point of view, can involve both being real-time, as in cellular devices, and in other than real-time using a WAP browser device that has access to the internet. Globility isn't just about engaging customers as they move about, it's about engaging customers from wherever they are.

This tremendous "mobilization" of consumers over the next several years becomes apparent when looking at any of the current market projections. Most credible forecasters expect that within two years the voice traffic on cellular devices will over take the voice traffic on wire-line devices. This is changing, for example, in North America at a rate of over some 65,000 new cellular subscribers a day. And, in a few short years after that, web traffic from WAP enabled browsers will over take web traffic from wire-line and broadband architectures.

It is entirely plausible to this futurist that within ten years as much as, if not more than, eighty percent of all internet traffic will be conducted over WAP browsers. The richness of combining the internet with mobile devices is so much more than simple applications such as stock quotes, flight updates, email, restaurant directions, and weather forecasts. There are now ads that say call this number and use your WAP browser.

The idea of WAP browsers is leading many to conceive of a world where companies can easily communicate offers, transaction information, and business intelligence to customers, agents, and salespeople. While mobile CRM is inevitable, there are several significant challenges to be overcome before we see mass adoption. Competing standards, preparing content in formats for presentation on different systems, deploying gateways to translate different communications protocols, the cost of integrating old customer data with new systems, and the most significant, the impact of application portability.

The amount of traffic that will be generated as a result of this mobile consumer means that if you don't have a multi-channel enabled call center, even for a small business of as few as ten telephones, you can't run your business. You cannot even have a contact center running, let alone and CRM focus in your business.

Globility has a dimension of enterprise applications as well. Increasingly, we are seeing enterprises becoming truly distributed and mobile. The Cahners In-Stat Group a Scottsdale, AZ based market research firm, estimates that by 2004 the average large corporation in the United States will support about 153 remote offices with 660 telecommuters and more than 29 million wireless-enabled workers.

Because of the sheer volume of calls that will drive this tremendous growth, traditional telecommunications applications will no longer be about controlling voice flow and connection on the enterprise premises, it will be about controlling communication globally. The interesting thing about IP is that it enables the ability to network people back to the enterprise at a level of one. This level of one can be somebody in a home, on a cell phone, or where ever they are. Ironically, the process begins with the networking of small business and business divisions. The granularity of teleworking is entirely dependant on the growth and penetration of succession networks.

In these corporate environments they need to have contact back to their offices, ideally through single number voice messaging and email, especially those companies with executives and employees traveling overseas. Although the technology to enable this is certainly available today, it is still functionally very difficult to use, much less make it all work together. There are enterprise-integrated cellular products today that can seamlessly shift from internal networks to carrier networks. In this scenario, an executive can walk into his office, never turning off his cell phone as it begins to work through the enterprise network, then leave the office and the cell phone starts to ring again.

Another dimension of the mobility of workers, better defined as remote working or teleworking, can readily be identified in the United States with the rapid spread of urbanization. A consequence of urbanization is the increasing distribution of labor workforces. Ironically, it is only in the last century that people began to work and travel to centralized offices; for the vast majority of human history, people worked out of their homes. Again, looking at call centers, we can see the impact of this workforce mobility technology.

It wasn't so long ago that companies would decide, for example, to put in a call center in Iowa because they could have access to cheap labor (and there was a lot of it). Now the call centers of today are where it requires the recruiting of technical experts and customer support people who make can make as much as $80,000 to $120,00 a year sitting in technical call centers. This population of knowledge-worker, or gold-collar worker, can demand to live exactly where they want to, not where the company they work for wants them to live. Quality-of-life demands fulfillment and it is one of the most underestimated issues, and benefits, of remote teleworking. The emergent mobile and remote working technologies will enable the employment of high-tech and skilled workers in localities and communities where they would choose to live, not where the company would choose for them to live. Offering to move a ski bum to Utah from the expensive California Bay Area becomes a powerful hiring and retention tool.

At one time, one particular large telecommunications company had a 100 person call center located in Burlington, VT. Using mobile and remote teleworking technology, they successfully disintermediated the physical call center while maintaining the same team of 100 people in the area. As networking and broadband technology develops, it is becoming increasingly more practical not only to have smaller and more remote call centers, but with emergent generation of network routing intelligence call centers are virtual and can be made up of singular locations in diverse places such as Florida, Texas, Utah, Washington, and Rhode Island.

For at least the next few years, there is going to be such a critical shortage of gold-collar workers that companies will be significantly hampered unless they have a strong and integrated remote teleworking arrangement. With mobility and distributed labor resource demands, teleworking becomes the most viable alternative and an evolutionary inevitability. The drag on the evolutionary pace of enabling a remote population of teleworkers will come from influences such as the enthusiastic adoption of broadband use, online education, and training.

Multi Channel Customer Relationship Management

The emergence of mobility and broadband connectivity has expanded the demands of multi-channel based customer relationships (as opposed to single channel such as the telephone or mail) to being not only a real-time demand for service, but a demand for the ability to handle multi-contacts with the customer in an integrated fashion. Mobility is not about engaging customers as they move about it's about engaging customers from wherever they are.

CRM is not just a single application, it is a series of applications working with definite business goals enabling a complete view of how the customer interacts with a company's products and service.

"Integrated" implies that the company has knowledge about what the customer has already done through different channels. This knowledge is applied to the routing of the contact to the most appropriate person because the company understands the different ways the customer has contacted it. It also implies that when a customer or prospect does successfully contact your company the enterprise is armed with information and the history of what that particular customer has been going through, regardless of how they have accessed the enterprise.

This further implies, from a management perspective, a need for very serious data and data analytics. This is discussed briefly later in this chapter.

CRM, Customer Relationship Management, is the ability to manage customer and enterprise information in real-time—real-time being defined as when the customer wants to contact your company and in the media that they prefer. This could be fax, FedEx, email, web collaboration, WAP browser, or mobile phone call. Regardless of the method, the customer demands to interact with you.

In one vision of the multi-channel CRM, real-time is simply a change in the dimension of service. It is no longer good enough to have real-time voice and it is no longer good enough to have real-time email or chat. Real-time demand for service is only good enough if the customer switches media and the enterprise can still manage the transaction with full knowledge of what the customer is doing, intending to do, or has already done.

This requires the contact with the customer to be integrated with a common data repository that centralizes and formats information on customers. And, the availability of this information must be very near real-time to be effective. If a valued customer has just left your company's web site in disgust and is now calling you on the telephone using a number that you didn't make very easy to find then an ideal integrated CRM plan will make it possible for an agent's console, regardless of their physical location, to display customer information in a format that makes that real-time agent aware of each of the previous engagements. For example, instantly an agent would be able to see that the customer was on the web site, they sent you an email, you responded with an email, they checked some more things out on the web site, and now they are calling on the phone. Seeing this series of transactions when customers' call would avoid, if not eliminate, much of the replicating customer information that occurs today.

CRM is the ability to respond with more than just responding in real-time.

The bigger challenge of CRM is managing what happens with a customer over a series of transactions (some believe that this should be a lifetime's worth). How do you coordinate the different interactions with customers across these different interaction channels? How do you insure that the customer gets handled in an intelligent way when the customer contacts you using this different media?

What we are finding today that accounts for this "gapping" is that in most enterprises the web response and the email response groups are often in and under the IT group's domain. E-contact is more often than not driven by somebody who is viewed as a technologist and has absolutely no relationship to the other customer contact channel found in the circuit voice-based call center. When you agree that both e-mail and voice have identical functions, you will also agree that they have the exact same mission, just in different media.

For example, the customer is on your website and they get completely disgusted and hang up and call you. You need to know about that. Or, the customer places an order on your web site, calls on the phone to confirm the order, and you send them a thank-you email. Then you need them to fill out a warranty card.

The ability to seamlessly move between a telephone call and a web site for assistance is the Holy Grail of CRM. The company that learns to use technology to engage customers proactively and seamlessly, will not only create lifetime value for the customer, but lifetime profit for the company.

It would stun this writer blind if I were to receive a proactive call from a company after I purchased their product to ask me if I got it assembled, installed, or working correctly. The power with loyalizing customers occurs when the company discovers that the customer is missing a red widget but hasn't had the time to call or arrange service or completion. While the company may think that the service loop is closed, the customer is still seeking closure. The company should be the one making the proactive contact and this requires multi-channel routing intelligence.

From a routing perspective, particularly of traditional voice-based applications even in the emerging discipline of eCRM, few vendors—no more than three or four—can actually provide sophisticated routing intelligence that includes circuit based voice applications. The idea of successful eCRM without integration with traditional voice circuits is absurd. The idea that traditional voice circuits will not ultimately be absorbed, converged with IP, is equally absurd. The concept that eCRM-based applications can run, or ever will run, on traditional PBX's is ridiculous. Over time, however, eCRM applications will likely grow to be standalone.

The Evolution of Voice Circuits

As convergence moves ahead, the core competence of providing the reliability of dial tone is a competitive differentiator and should be a prime consideration in vendor and partner selection.

Business over IP is really just a buzzword for trying to describe voice as an application. The difficulty in actually managing the ability to forward a simple telephone call is tremendously underestimated. Fairly traditional applications, such as an executive or call center agent being able to manage their call coverage, are terribly complex to execute on IP platforms today.

Soft-phones, screen pop, email integration, intelligent look-ahead routing, network interqueue, remote agents skill assignments, mix-media queue control, customize reporting, work force management, and redundant application servers are examples of the many sophisticated voice applications that enterprises take for granted. The competitive difference today between the vendors of this technology is their being able to provide these "taken-for-granted" applications and run them over the customer's network of choice.

Most of the IP evolutionary drag comes from the fear that traditional voice based PBX's are proprietary. When a quick-witted industry analyst Shelia McGee Smith suggests that today's PBX's are mostly just "proprietary mainframes," it should be pointed out that there is not likely a software applications vendor today, at least in North America, where a current version of any PBX couldn't be fully integrated in less than thirty days. The reason that this doesn't happen has more to do with competitive commerce than integration ability.

There are significant unintended consequences as a result of relying too much on analysts and consultants who rarely have access to the true internal spending data of a technology vendor. They never really know, at least until after the fact, how research and development dollars are allocated and hence don't know where impactful technologies will be developed. Today, I estimate that at least 80 percent of the traditional telecom vendor's research and development investment is in software which is contrary to the expectation that there should be more of an investment in hardware.

Unfortunately, market observers and analysts do not know how much off-the-shelf and standard technology actually will be used, mostly because this is something that vendors don't often advertise. The fact is, if you crawl through any PBX today you will find industry standard components. There is a tremendous amount of standard software in use today.

The evolved PBX today is one where it is a pure application architecture—where voice is just an application. And this voice ability becomes more of an application as we move into the future and so portability becomes a critical factor. What travels and transports with that voice application is a deeply embedded, even cultural, expectation of reliability. Contrasting the reliability expectations that exist between circuits and packets is still dramatic.

Voice applications on PBXs won't go away anytime soon because of the reality that IP based products are not reliable enough, don't have the features and mobility end-users really want, and still do not scale.

The economics for IP are not eating away at the economics of circuits quite as fast as popular and trade media would have us believe. Cisco, for example, propagandizes that companies can save huge amounts of money by putting their voice networks on the data networks, which is consistently not true. Still today, in many cases, companies end up spending more money

But there will be places in the enterprise where this technology could be potentially useful and they are certainly going to experiment with it. Over time, such as a ten-year period, we could look at the technology of ISDN as proof-point.

The truth is voice today is already just an application that happens to run on a proprietary mainframe requiring millions of lines of code—most of which is legacy code—and as a consequence, is a little bit more complicated.

In this world of convergence, people overlook and take for granted the massive support and infrastructure required just to provide dial tone. Dial tone has created an expectation of communications that will never change. At least the expectation never lowers—people notice when it fails.

Today, CRM decisions should, at minimum, be influenced by whether technology vendors make part of that network infrastructure or not. What successful companies will do and where their focus should be is on the services and solutions. Technology partners should be focused on application solution-ing with a clear design and ability to migrate to any platform, at any time. This application portability of voice will become a global competitive differentiator.

Application Portability

The minute an enterprise makes a decision that they are multi-channeled or e-enabled (the minute that *you* make that decision) they have made the decision to dis-integrate with the circuit and integrate with the packet. Email, for example, is here to stay while the telephone isn't going away anytime soon. The concept of application portability is defined intrinsically as the ability to run applications on a circuit switch or port it to IP, or run it on both, simultaneously.

The advantage to a customer being able to run an application on both simultaneously is significant. Contrary to the media hype that companies are rapidly ripping out their circuit switches and replacing them with IP for voice applications, the fact of the matter is that most are doing so because they can use their data network—you cannot do this on a PBX.

You cannot do this on a system that is optimized for voice. It must be done on a system that is optimized for IP. And you have to do it on a system that works with the applications that already exist in the business.

What is important as part of the concept of application portability is the cost of the software, not the cost of the server. Servers no longer cost very much in today's world, relatively speaking. The true cost is in having to port the enterprise's applications from generation to generation, from server to server. Cost is now in the software itself and not necessarily in the cost of the integration, although integration expenses can occasionally get out of hand.

The impact of application portability is no longer on technology but the impact on your business, your customers, and the disruption in training of employees.

So, when an enterprise builds an application that tracks customer interactions over time to route these engagements in real-time based on media and collects data on all of these transactions be it voice, email, web chat, or web help, the idea of application portability requires intelligence in the routing. We can find this in the analytics of customer data.

Data Mining

CRM is fundamentally based on collecting data and managing information about customer transactions over time. Data mining's promise is to be able to slice, dice, chew, and digest massive terabytes of data about customers and their likely behavior at and with every engagement. Such insights can be used to improve service, increase response rates, and retain customers.

Most CRM applications today are made up of workflow rules that run on top of a CRM engine or customer data repository and support front office employees and call center agents. Sales force automation, professional service applications, incident handling systems, and opportunity management systems are the four primary internally focused CRM applications. An important distinction of front office applications is that they are channel independent, meaning that they support employees rather than the customer directly. They rely heavily on the customer data repository and are often looked at as systems that offer execution support for maximizing the lifetime value of each customer to the enterprise.

Just a few short years ago, business analytics would have been, for example, an electronic components company identifying the top ten products bought by each customer and the ten least-popular products. Then they would transfer this data from the back-office system (accounting) to the front-office system (the call center) for call center initiatives. We have come some ways since, as this is what technology now enables.

There is a critical emergent market sector here related to data and information analytics. This also implies an ability to start to track and understand the lifetime value of your customers and how this value changes over time because now technology can track and graphically display customer behaviors over a series of interactions using a variety of different media. The consequence of this mining for rich correlations in data amongst media is much more than the information we can typically derive from a traditional call center. In a traditional voice-based call center environment, all the enterprise can really see is a certain snapshot in time based on an algorithm and metric called Erlang.

The application of data mining manifests itself economically when the remote worker or call center agent has a console where they can see the information and the flow of customer engagements. From a single screen, the enterprise can identify that the customer was on the web site (twice), they sent them an email, you responded with an email, they checked some more things out on the web site, and now they are calling on the phone. This console gives them a set of information about how the customer accessed them and what pages they have been on and the totality of their emails. Seeing this series of transactions when the customer calls avoids much of the service interaction slow-down that occurs today.

A key function of any emergent business analytics applications will be the ability to not only track all of these different types of media, but route them as well. Be cautioned that inhaling tons of customer data and then spitting out cheesy offers through every channel possible does not make a relationship.

The complexity of analytics available today is far more than the market can support at the moment, however uptake will match complexity in as little as 18 months. The reality of data mining today is that it can certainly be done, but expensively. Implementation of large-scale software applications can take months before skills are developed enough to extract any usable information.

Change is Hard and Slow

Convergence is another word for hybridization. Both actually happen at a slow evolutionary pace, not a rapid one. The uptake and adoption of technology does not happen as quickly as the media or the manufacturers of that technology would want us to believe. And when the adoption of technology does occur, it occurs in fits and starts as well.

Technology is an evolution for business and enterprises because they have big investments, the smaller of the investments actually being in the technology and the larger in what it means and how it is used for the business. It is no longer about technology because there are a lot of good technology companies out there all ready.

This is a perfect business case for getting away from ROI—return on investment—and getting into return on intelligence and information.

Application focus is a market segment descriptor, a certain type of a philosophy, that describes a unique emerging demand for technology uses that are now more oriented toward return-on-information instead of the traditional return-on-investment. For years, the bell-head mentality has driven a scrutiny of application impact based on cost and investment (ROI). Now, Siemens is supporting a message that has a broader appeal throughout the enterprise including up to the c-level. Yes, you still must maintain a relationship with the switch administrator in the closet in the basement, but if you are not selling to higher up people who think and care about workforce productivity and the customer relationship management, you will fail. It is at this level where the bigger impact is.

Traditionally IT departments, having a line gauge in traditional cost accounting, do not take the impact of changing technology and applications sufficiently into account. More than the psychic cost of a loss of productivity by employees, the bigger impact is the one on your customers. If we were talking about help desks and other employees this would be one case, but in most cases the impact is at the service level in the service department or an inside sales department where the payback numbers over time are huge.

Solutioning

> **so-lu•tion•ing** \sə-lü-shen-iŋ\ *n* : the ability to design, implement, and support a comprehensive solution and do it globally. Requires application portability.

There are a handful of companies today that can be the expert in multi-channel routing, multi-channel data collection, and a certain level of the customer relationship management. But CRM is too complex for any one vendor and most companies out there have investments in Quintas, Calrify, Vantive, Remedy, Siebel, SAP, and all of the voice and telecom vendors, all of whom are optimize for the different parts of the customer relationship.

A significant portion of the ROI of any CRM application must be based on the application's portability. To successfully manage relationships with its customers, companies will have to master not only application and information portability across multiple channels in an intelligent manner, but portability between vendors.

CRM, perhaps more than any other information technology initiative of the past thirty years, has been more misunderstood or underestimated. Nothing has been more pervasive on the effect on enterprise since the ideas and theories of efficiency guru Fredrick Taylor.

CRM is not software, it is not a project or mission statement. CRM is a business operating system and a failure to understand this will ensure failure to achieve a return on investment, not to mention a return on relationship.

The meta-vision of globility and solutioning demands a goal, ultimately in a real-time CRM environment, both for the enterprise's agents and systems and for the company's customers. CRM demands the responsibility—the ability to respond from wherever they are—as well as the ability to pull data from everywhere the enterprise does any kind of business, analyze it, and send it to agents as needed to encourage sales, ease procurement, and resolve problems.

Combining the front end of CRM and its back end analytical side with the demands of the smarter mobile enabled customer and we can identify a natural evolution toward corporate intelligence where combining the thought mining of employee opinions and ideas with the data mining of historical customer data creates returns on relationships that last a lifetime, even generations.

Chapter Nine
Succession Networks

"We've heard that a million monkeys at a million keyboards could produce the complete works of Shakespeare; now, thanks to the internet, we know that is not true." – Robert Wilensky

Cloud Impact

Call centers are a proof point for the pragmatic application of technology. Networking technology is no exception, particularly within the still vast circuits of voice networking. If a technology or specifically an application of technology is not found in a call center, it is likely not a very practical technology. The technology of global telecommunications networks is no exception.

We can look precisely at call centers and understand how quickly new devices, interfaces and applications are being accepted by the masses are actually being accepted.

Few vertical technology issues gets so little attention, but have as much of the influence on the evolutionary pace of technology as that of the emerging next generation of networks. An understanding the true nature and underestimated impact of these emerging succession networks inevitably ends up changing conventions on how we think the applications of technology will customer service.

One of the paradoxes and dilemmas of the service disciplines such as CTI, CRM, ERP and so on attract, is that they will not happen any faster that the networks that support these application, devices and interfaces develop. In this chapter we look at the emerging succession network(s) and conclude that the pace of the network evolution is the same as the pace of the customer service management evolution. Unfortunately, this pace is happening a little slower in general than most people anticipate.

The evolutionary next few stages of CRM will happen only at the pace of the development of emergent succession networks. These succession networks, at the moment, are not developing quite as fast as application disciplines such as data-mining, searching and knowledge database.

Evolution is happening at almost nearly the exact pace as the developers of technology that supports the large networks are developing, selling and implementing. In fact that we are already well into the transition to fiber optic based carrier networks is borne out by the fiber optic market strengths of companies such as Siemens.

The biggest influence from the emergence of fiber optical (Gildercosmic) based networks, is that today enterprises and organizations are now starting to actually take orders and constructing networks parallel to their voice networks – these are the succession networks. Why what happens with the development and implementation of these succession networks is important, critical in fact, is because demand generation and it's fulfillment, will come from and through these very networks.

These succession networks will not only carry information, but applications will be added to this dumb glass to create intelligence. This intelligence will now be spread throughout the entire customer demand chain tremendously affecting how, where and when enterprise's interact with it's customers. The idea of globility and application portability, discussed in Chapter 8, requires succession to more intelligent networks.

The intelligence of the succession networks acutely effects the service companies provide through their customer service operations, notably the call centers. Understanding the pace of the rollout of these succession networks provides powerful insight into the pace the emergence of CRM and customer service related applications.

Gaining a return on relationships is predicated on the assumption that there is intelligence that flows between customer and company at every engagement. The flow of this intelligence is influenced by the ability of communicate as much information between the two as necessary and as possible. This requires not only smart devices such as PCs, cell phones and PDAs, but smart connections between the two. If you want to understand the pace of change of the technology and applications of customer service, understand the pace of change of the succession networks that this change will happen over and through.

The Pace of the Race

North American culture, on whole does not change their interfaces or networks quite as quickly as the popular mass media would have us to believe. Pundits claim that high bandwidth, smart applications and devices are going to start coming on line within two years, by 2002.

And while this seems a little unrealistic and will more likely occur over a ten year period, we can be certain that there will become little or no difference between public networks and large enterprise networks. With the exception of the possibility that governments get involved in carrier networks for profit, most all companies at some level will all be carriers of information, data, signals and messages.

As for hardware, the architecture and the components in the public networks are converging toward the same thing as the architecture and components found in enterprise networks. Within this period of time Cisco will likely develop telephony grade reliability in it's product line and the bellheads will have optimized for packet based data. In those Large organizations that run their own networks, the platforms will be the same as those of the telephone companies.

The largest deposit of copper to be found in the world still remains New York City. These new emerging succession networks have plenty of copper-based circuits out on the edge where the individual consumer is. While the core of the network expands on a backbone of fiber based IP and ATM (asynchronous transfer mode) packets.

Likely these succession networks will have thick very high-speed backbones that are ATM and IP based addressing further out on the edges. On the fringes of the network capillary forces will be drawn through copper in the form of DSL and cable modems and eventually wireless. We will see an ATM interior, an IP periphery and copper/wireless edge.

This always growing succession network of packets will function metaphorically much like a power transmission grid. When there is excess or limited capacity, arbitrage mechanisms fluidly enable individuals and companies to put in and pull out network capacity.

This is admittedly a gross simplification. The end-users of bandwidth do not call up or place an order for the bandwidth they require at the moment. This arbitrage for bandwidth may never happen at the end-user level, it will remain something that likely happens between the main network carriers. At the outside edge the arbitrage of bandwidth is transparent to the end-user; it does not happen on the desktop, it happens in the router.

However, from an end-user perspective, the ones generating the demanding what happens is something completely opposite. At the networks edge users think they have all of the bandwidth they could possibly ever want; nearly free and on all of the time. From the end-user consumer perspective, what drives people into these high bandwidth competitive options will be the cost of service, the quality of the service and the reliability of the service.

Ironically, these telephony grade rule are the same rules that clearly are governing the true uptake pace of IP telephony.

In it's current form, the internet is a just a prototype of the succession type network. Ultimately succession networks start off looking much like the internet excepting that most enterprises become involved in some form of arbitraging the increasingly massive amount of available bandwidth becomes available.

Many companies are not oblivious to the potential of generating revenue streams from carrying publicly available data over it's private networks. There are already many large, global financial institutions, for example, that are in a sense wholesale data carriers. In some cases these enterprises are applying for and obtaining the necessary licenses to become network class carriers because what they do already for their own operations, already evidenced in call center applications, they can arbitrage to the general market for revenue.

There's No Time for Negotiation

One of the reasons that the communication between customers and companies is the way that it is, is because there is no time to exchange much information before the actual engagement begins. Because of the limitation of network intelligence, the intelligence that goes into call centers is based on very limited information. Identifying a ten digit phone number is much different than figuring out exactly what a caller wants.

Succession networks enable network intelligence. The application of this available intelligence is that companies and customers will be able to have a meta-data conversation before the actual engagement occurs. When you have intelligence in the end points communicating through intelligent networks, a tremendous amount of negotiation will happen fast enough that the focus of the engagement by the company can be qualitative.

Today we can find a precursor to the conceptual information exchange that succession networks enable. II, Information Indicator, the two digit signal from the network about the type of call; pay phone, cell phone or prison for example, is form pre-contact exchange of information.

Application examples of this meta-data conversation would be; The customer speaks English and you speak French. Meta-data negotiates to do the translation, in text, in the communication layer with x protocol. If you get out there even further, you can foresee applications where eventually the negotiation of meta-data about a customer's credit history (why show a customer a BMW, when all they can afford is a Pontiac?) and lifestyle preferences takes place. The Holy Grail of one to one marketing is the ability to execute customer pricing discrimination based on forecasted demands of customer preferences. Technology enables more information to be swapped, traded and bartered so that customer demands can be better fulfilled.

Increasingly we will see devices and interfaces that talk comfortably with Siemens technology, but not easily with Siebel applications. An intelligent transaction between company and customer will require translation to happen in a communications layer between the two applications– the cloud, before the customer must initiate any type of action such as using IVR, accessing a web site or talking to a call center agent.

When these high bandwidth succession networks with plenty intelligent devices out on the ends arrive, intelligent endpoints will be negotiating the for the actual communication medium and protocols. Customer engagements will be initiated by the near automatic decisions about who is the best carrier to use at that moment and when the customer connects, for example to an agent (real or virtual) that the customer can define in advance the language spoken. The customer-initiator of the engagement will be able to tell the enterprise what kind of device or devices are being used and what kind of protocol these devices understand.

On the enterprise's CRM application side, the enterprise intelligence will be tuned to the identification of the customer and a description of their requirements. This is perhaps more clearly identified as a demand unit, the data unit structures that are used to run every business. Every customer focused company, particularly if there is a call center facet, will have a metalanguage, a way to describe each and every contact. Through this metalanguage the customer and the enterprise will able to exchange information. This information becomes an instant part of the engagement creation and service fulfillment routines.

So, not only does the medium become transparent, but the end points are where the intelligence resides become transparent as well. The intelligent endpoints can communicate intelligence over networks because they have the available bandwidth. From the enterprise perspective, what they have done is write a description of the widget and they say they are willing to communicate with video and the meta-data becomes completely transparent to the users.

In one service application scenario, the customer tell the phone company that they want to buy a watch. The phone company will connect me to somebody who can sell me a watch. If I happen to have a Microsoft package on my PC that I am using to manage my personal finances and that watch company happens to have Clarify running its front office and behind Clarify there is a whole bunch of other things, that negotiation will happen in the network. In fact, ultimately, depending how privacy issues evolve, the end user may never even know about this meta- exchange.

Customers now tell the company exactly what they want, how they speak, how they pay and how they want it shipped. From over the succession networks will come all sorts of information available even before the customer has made a connection. This succession network will support populating an agents screen, not with just pre-existing customer information, but with real-time information related to that particular transaction.

This idea of pro-acted intelligence over intelligent succession networks changes the entire call center universe tremendously.

From this we are evolving to a condition where customers have as much access to the same information as the call center agent does, in many cases more information than the agents themselves. From over the succession networks much of the information collection that agents used to do, they no longer have to do. All of the work takes place from the PC on, not from the human on. The agent no longer makes the decisions about the need to speak in English, the customer wants a watch, I want to use this credit card and I am using this particular kind of interface. People no longer have to negotiate these kinds of things.

Already today we see an application bias toward customers first trying to engage a transaction themselves without any other persons involvement. Theoretically the load on the agents should be less in this model. Then they will be saying, "here is what I want to do, exactly why they are calling and how they want to be handled." A lot of what we are doing in call centers now, besides trying to keep people entertained and happy while they are waiting to get a live person, I am trying to anticipate why they are calling. This goes away. Most of the problems implementing is trying to anticipate why the customer is calling.

The evolutions happening in the network is reflected by the evolutions happening at the end points, specifically in call centers. In the past companies have enabled people to become experts at speed and efficiencies. Today industry thought leaders are actually leading initiatives to get away from enabling technologies that support expertise-ness in efficiencies, as opposed to expertise-ness with customer relationships.

The paradigm is truly shifting here, although it is important to express that enterprise's shouldn't not be interested in efficiencies. The evolving definition of efficiency is in meeting business goals, it is not in saving time. The fact is that the fundamental ideas of CRM contradicts the efficiencies companies strive to achieve in call centers and with their customers today. The intelligence to be found in the succession networks will radically change the whole notion of what a call center or customer contact center.

Mixing Oil, Web and Water

On a practical and pragmatic level, traditional customer interaction technologies such as Interactive Voice Response (IVR) provide for basic level routing; caller triaging based on the most rudimentary of information. IN the succession networks the exchange of information before the engagement occurs forces things such as IVR menus to simply go away. The decision tree routing that IVRs are designed to do is done before the contact is made by the caller.

The intelligently enabled succession networks will be able to mix and deliver the valuable kind of information that enterprises traditionally get from CRM applications with the operational efficiencies squeezed from IVRs and ACDs.

The inevitability of growth being slowed by a reluctance to change quite as quickly as popular media would have us believe that fundamental customer application technologies such as IVR and CTI are deeply rooted in expectations and service processes of every enterprise today. In spite of an overwhelming business case for it, the predictive dialing market is a fairly contentious market space. Preview for call backs is an import part of the equation, campaign management is important and proactive personalization is extremely important. Contact management without a proactive form of engagement with the customer is like yin without a yang.

Nobody wants call centers, they want business processes. Nobody wants ACD or IVRs, they have a sales problems or a customer support problem they want to solve and the only way to solve it is to view this from a larger that traditional perspective. Now we have the ability to provide tools to measure the customer facing activities and touch points objectives that are in line with how you want to measure relationship. If you think that it is important to get customers to use your IVR, but they keep zeroing out, maybe there is a problem with your IVR.

If you look at what the emerging technology pieces are today, like the IVR and the speech enabled applications that do what an IVR does.

Because we have the touch points and the data base where it all goes we are going to take this information and tell the customer if they are meeting their objectives, the service missions. Just to get a little closer to what we are doing now, we take that personalization of the touch points.

In the case of the call center we already have the IVR we already have the personalization of the touch points because we write the call center scripts and we write the IVR applications. Take this information out of the database and then you can then define what a good customer relationship is to you, the customer, and then you can create plans based on the value of those relationships and what you want to do with those relationships.

These on-the-fly plans become implementable with every engagement regardless of media. Intelligent networks will route calls, customize IVR and web page options. Regardless is it is a PC, WAP browser or on board computer, intelligent exchange will ensure the precise advertisements the customer wants to be exposed to, be this audio on-hold or audio on-line.

There powerful internal consequences of creating perpetual closed-loop CRM. Every time the customer phone call gets handed to an agent we are going to add some information to the CRM database about what happened to that engagement before it got to the agent or the next web page.

When any information is captured and is fed are back into correctly tuned CRM databases, agent performance metrics emerge based on relationship objectives, not just Erlanged length of calls. When an enterprise, specifically in its call centers, evolves from being focused on the length of customer calls, to the length of it's customer relationships, it hits stride with the philosophical demands of customer managed relationships and CRM.

Analytics

The idea that managing the demands of customers for a return on these relationships requires some serious analytics and data mining. Within the ever burgeoning chaos of data and information overflow emerge patterns of customer behavior. Serious attention needs to be paid to the disciplines that combine the predictions of behavior with the information targeting of marketing to create offers that are tailored to specific customers.

The analytics piece of returns on relationships and solutioning occurs when profound trends or spikes are found. Clustering and defining who valuable customer are is the mission. What succession networks enable is an instant decision, a routing or prioritization based on what is a good relationship or what is a bad relationship at the time.

From a web front end to a customer phone call, data mining and analytics are the disciplines that define who are desired customers and who are less desired, at any moment. Without analytics companies can not establish customer value so they can then create pricing discrimination.

The challenge is how to take the different kinds of definitions about the return on customer relationships; what is a good relationship, turn it into something that is implementable and feed that information back into the enterprise; back into the routing systems and back into the reporting systems.

CRM systems never had this information before and the ACD never had the information in the CRM system and so now enterprises can implement business rules that for example say; "Even though the company computes that this customer is not worth a lot of money, however the last time he called, we made him wait for twenty minutes. Since we have agents available in twenty seconds, let's this time let's treat to a gold customer level of service."

Using intelligence delivered across these succession networks, the enterprise's customer analytics engine has all of the knowledge about what the contact, the desk-top, the x-top, the voice-top web-top application ought to look like. What it needs to take an order, what it needs to provide customer support, Clarify has all of that information. They know what these application look like and they know how to customize these applications and how to provide the end users with tools to develop these applications in such a way that it is maintainable when they upgrade from one version of software to the next. They have figured out this problem. We have figured out how to do ACD, routing, reporting and real-time statistics back to those things.

Without a functional database for the analytics to chew on, the value of the information to really make any kind of meaningful decisions about routing in any medium becomes null.

When Networks Change Agents Change

The evolutionary changes in the network intelligence force the evolution of the agents as well. This influences the role of the agent to change as well.

Certainly most of the drudgery found in call centers today, the kind responsible for ridiculously high turnover rates, will be taken over by the technology. Most of traditional call center agents do today will be automate out of existence.

To be clear, humans will not be automated out of existence; this comes much later. As pure knowledge-workers, agents becomes an expert in something, a researcher who has a better resources to depend on for bandwidth enabled collaborative engagements.

From the intelligence exchanged over these succession networks, the enterprise will know everything I ever need to know about this calling customer before they are even connected to an agent. When the customer initiates the engagement, the agent is no longer driving the conversation anymore. The agent is more like a consultant who is helping the customer solve his own problem.

There are two pervasive dangers here to rushing into the perceived richness of analytics and data-mining. One is the inflexibility of Erlang based traditional service metrics and the other is that technology is often still too complex for the people that use it.

The good new – bad news about the fundamentals of telecommunications technology today is pretty clear. With one hand the big vendors build technology that enables massive and ingrained population of people who are experts at Erlang. With the other hand they enable the forward thinking CRM applications that discard the metrics of Erlang in light of the fact that Erlang fundamentally contradicts what a return on relationship strives to achieve.

Siemens, Nortel, Avaya and others are appropriately moving away from the traditional notions and metrics of Erlang. The fact of the matter is that in the enterprises today that are working on CRM initiatives they are stuffing the productivity reports in their desks. CRM means they just don't care about average talk time or sales per hour.

CRM forces technology to evolve to tracking and measuring just efficiencies. If an agent is on a call for three hours with a prospective customer one day, exchanges several emails tha next, chats on another and three days later that very customer places a million dollar order, you want to give the agent credit for being on the phone for that three hours.

Another danger of the pervasivness of technology, manifest in call centers specifically is one of the effect of Siebelism. Siebelism defines when a technology's user interface becomes more complex than the people that use are capable of. The counter productive influence of Siebel-like technology may actually slow and inhibit market growth. Spending $5,000 per seat for complex technology and paying $7 per hour people to use it may not work. Particularly in call centers when companies start throwing technology at agent desktops, we simply be making smarter slaves. In the case of technology, it's application or even its intelligence; a rising tide does not float all boats.

Eventually intelligence in the networks make sup for the shortcomings of Erlangs and Siebelsims. What actually gets eliminated here is the complexity. Intelligence across these succession networks enables simplifying the customer to enterprise engagement. Enterprises will eventually get rid of the complexity and get back to the qualitative part of the engagement with the customer.

Now, Soon and Later The Pace of the Race

So the aforementioned applications may be stretching customer service fantasy a bit. Succession networks require vast amounts of unmitigated and available high bandwidth for me to do the kinds of applications that everybody is fanaticizing over.

Conversations at the carriers levels about the long term vision, a gap occurs between the long-term vision of three years and customers that are thinking about seven to ten year vision. Often at the enterprise level in the mean time, the product development cycles of 18 months can be last forever when measured in web cycles. The pace of the race is such that 18 months can mean three product or platform revisions.

Within the executive bowls of huge telecommunications companies introducing products, applications or platforms that are more than 18 months out, doesn't get any attention. In product development cycle anything more than 18 months cannot reflect that things will change so much between now and then.

At the end user level we are pragmatically looking at ten years be for we see appreciable impact of the succession networks. This can be tough for a companies that breath 36 month cycles. The truth of the matter is that a lot of this stuff that people are talking about happening in 18 months I don't think is going to happen in three years.

For intelligence across succession networks to emerge, a subtle chicken and egg thing must work itself out. Assuming that it will be five year before these networks are actually here, then calculate that it maybe much longer before the applications that take advantage of the networks are actually here themselves.

Not only do populations of end users not change their interfaces quite as quickly as mass media would have us believe, but the companies that will build the back bones of the succession network don't change so fast themselves, in spite of only mediocre mid-range vision.

You have all of these visionary people out there who are trying to do stuff now, or at least trying to do funding to this stuff, but it is not really happening. RosettaNet, the XML backbone (this is an XML based ability to interoperate between completely disparate systems, platforms and applications) has been around for more than five years and it is not really gaining any momentum. Whether or not it can gain momentum in the intervening five years from here to then remains to be seen. All of the arguments against why every company shouldn't be standardized on protocols such as RosettNet will certainly be gone in three to five years from now.

There are many companies, enterprises and technically advanced units within companies that are trying rudimentary intelligent exchange. Well financed green field start-ups are exploring in this space. However, none will be successful until the infrastructure is there. Part of the drag on emergent succession networks will be the infrastructure and connectivity. Today WAN is still very expensive per user. Once we get to the point where the price performance of bandwidth decreases at twice as fast as Moore's Law, this will become a non-issue.

Solutioning

The enablers of deeply affecting customer relationship technology, the partners to the enterprise and companies that actually have to make this stuff work. When you are choosing a vendor, or if you are developing new applications with old partners, be acutely aware of the emerging demand for solutioning.

Solutioning is response to the challenge in today's world where a customer may have diparate applications; Siemens HiPath and Quintas analytics. An enterprise will likely have a Clarify engine integrated with a Siemens HiPath. The first steps toward succession networks is obtaining complete integratability among products and applications, integration so seamless and operationally entangled that unhooking applications becomes more difficult that getting them to work together. This is defined as application portability in a previous chapter.

Application portability requires moving to a distributed network model so that every customer facing application or routine is also a CTI application. The future of technology is in application blocks that can be adapted and moved around. Solutioning is taking a bunch of building blocks that all work closely together and breaking them up into services. Everything becomes a service application and can be moved from platform to platform, or vendor to vendor. Things like ACD reporting, web site impressions and statistics generation get taken out. Today all of this basically just a bunch of C++ APIs. In the future the likely protocol for all of this will be CORBA like.

Network Succession Means Bell-Head Morphisis

In the convergence toward the succession networks, application portability, solutioning and intelligent exchange of information won't likely come from the phone company side of things.

The big telecommunications companies with maternalistic lineage to Ma Bell won't eventually fail because of what they do badly, they will fail because they don't stop doing what they do do well when it is no longer appropriate (ISDN, circuits and dial-up as examples). This will be hardest thing for the bell head who has a vision but still wants to run it like Bell. Because of this there will be many people who understand where this has to go, but will fail anyway. There is a lot of bell heads that are going to fail but will remain standing at the end of the day. They will swallow their learnings and just buy somebody that has actually succeeded in this space.

In the bellhead versus bithead discussions, ultimately the ones who win are the ones who have got the vision. The ones who are making the right investment decisions today. There are still some pretty clever people in the telephone side of the world. They have lot of money and a lot of muscle and it will emerge that they will try to do all of this stuff and will likely fail, but they probably be able to buy the people that succeed. The carriers will eventually be able to acquire their success and that the ASP will actually be a carrier. Whether or not the existing carriers are successful at getting in to this market or not depends how the merger and acquisition games ultimately play out.

What the telephone has enabled for the last one hundred years is business communications systems and then this became a complex and sophisticated digital telephone, but still a telephone. What the traditional telecommunications companies have left out is all of the applications that go around, not just the telephone, but every other potential end-user device or interface.

Two to five years from now it will easy and cheap for people to get giga-bits worth of connectivity. When this happens what used to be a central office environment, which is all of a heterogeneous environment made of up very specialized high speed data technology along with the traditional voice technology, all of this is going to be an IP infrastructure. There will be no difference between a central office and a data center.

Looking into the future, when succession networks are really just sophisticated data networks, the communications piece isn't likely to be a telephone. The devices sitting on the desks of employees and the devices in the hands of your customer will likely be considered to be just another voice enabled CRM portal. After this is what the telephone is against the backdrop of these emerging networks. And because it is the most prevalent device and will remain so for many years to come, the Bell progeny, and their strategic market approach, will continue to own the dominate influence in the pace of emergent succession networks.

Meta-Sight

The impact of the emergent succession networks on the application of customer service will be profound. This is obvious. What is not so obvious is how and where the balance of power will shift as a handful of dominant vendors race on competitively.

Racing parallel to the application of Customer relationship Management is the transition to networks of unlimited band width. Until succession network arrive that are capable of intelligently exchanging information, intelligence will remain in the endpoints, the devices that consumers use and the interfaces that agents use on their desk tops. IVR systems reflect a repetitive and primitive form of this information exchange, itself limited to the information shared through touch-tones.

With succession networks comes a change in the fundamental ways of performing computing, sharing information and collaborating. The devices at the edge are continuing to get smarter, but what this means is that when you have that really high network bandwidth, a part from being able to do television and these kinds of applications what you will be able to do in your communication will be able to have communication protocols that have much more meta-data associated with them.

Today, CRM is really nothing more that a glorified ACT or Goldmine application, a glorified contact management system that is specialized for all different kinds of contact. There is a lot of confusion about what CRM companies actually provide. What they want to provide requires much more intelligent exchange of information than enterprise are not even near to accomplishing today. Most customer service applications today really only manage the point of contact.

What succession networks will enable is the end of asking customers who they are and how they plan to pay. When you capture every element of engagement information and merge it with the contact management database, the web browser portal environment, the speech and language recognition environment and can put this all together, this is solutioning.

Emergent succession networks will enable the intelligent exchange of information between company and customer. As a consequence the evolutionary pace of change of the application disciplines such as CRM are more influenced by ability for devices to exchange and communicate information (WAP), than by the ability of devices to store information (cell phones and PCs). Managing and solutioning for this emerging and profound available intelligence requires meta-sight over the burgeoning media customers increasingly demand to use.

About the Author

Paul Anderson

paulanderson@houston.rr.com
paulandersonwrites.com

Paul Anderson is a ghostwriter, author, speaker and futurist who writes about and works with clients to develop strategies that take advantage of new communication technologies in this emerging age of access and information. In addition to consulting and ghostwriting for industry leaders, Mr. Anderson has written and authored numerous reports, white papers and articles. He has participated in many conferences on the technologies of customer relationships. He is the Forward Thinking columnist for Customer Interface Magazine and sits on its Editorial Advisory Board. Mr. Anderson sits and suffers on the Board of Directors for several technology start-up companies as well.

He is known for his pragmatic perspective, provocative presentations and published best-selling books; *A Call From the 21st Century, The Technology of Customer Contact* and *The Digital Call Center; Gateway to Technical Intimacy.* His recently completed book, *The Executive's Guide to Customer Relationship Management; Loyalty, Retention, Profits* is in its third edition and is used in several university curriculums on technology marketing.

Year 2000 clients included Siemens ICN, Nortel Networks, SBC Global Networks, Avaya, Blue Pumpkin, CMP Media and Advanstar.